EVERYTHING YOU NEED TO KNOW ABOUT

GEOGRAPHY
HOMEWORK

ANNE ZEMAN

KATE KELLY

AN IRVING PLACE PRESS BOOK

SCHOLASTIC REFERENCE

Cover design, Red Herring Design; Cover illustration, Sarajo Frieden
Interior design, Bennett Gewirtz, Gewirtz Graphics, Inc.; Interior illustration, Greg Paprocki

Grateful acknowledgment is made to:
NASA for permission to reprint photograph on page 9.

Library of Congress Cataloging-in-Publication Data

Zeman, Anne, 1952–
Everything you need to know about Geography homework / Anne
Zeman and Kate Kelly.
p.   cm.—(Scholastic homework reference series)
Includes index.
ISBN 0-439-62546-7
1. United States—History—Miscellanea—Juvenile literature.
2. Homework—Juvenile literature. [1. United States—History.
2. Homework.] I. Kelly, Kate. II. Title. III. Series.
E178.3.Z45   1994
973—dc20

AC

10 9 8 7 6 5 4 3 2   05 06 07 08 09

Printed in the U.S.A.
First Printing this Edition, January 2005

Contents

Part 4. Plants and Animals

Part 5. People on Land and Water

Appendix

Index

It's time to do your homework—but you have questions. You need some help, but no adults are around, and you can't reach your classmates on the phone. Where can you go for help?

What Questions Does This Book Answer?

In *Everything You Need to Know About Geography Homework*, you will find a wealth of information, including answers to some of the most commonly asked geography homework questions, like

• Why do particular regions have different climates and what kinds of climates are there? The world's climate regions, or biomes, are described on pages 51–56.

• How do clouds affect climate? The effect of clouds on climate is explained on page 49.

• Why do we have seasons? Seasons are described on page 14.

• Where can I find descriptions of the U.S. states, including nicknames, state name origins, populations, and capital cities? "The U.S. in Focus," found on page 117, provides this type of information and more.

• How can latitude and longitude be used to locate major cities and other features on Earth? An explanation on how to use the geographic grid, which is formed by lines of latitude and longitude, is found on page 12.

• What are the different parts on a standard map? The parts of a standard map, including scale, compass, index, legends, and dates, are illustrated and defined on pages 26–29.

• What are the longest rivers in the world? The longest rivers in the world are listed and located on a map on pages 40–41.

• What are the names of the layers of the earth? A diagram describing the layers of the earth is found on page 30.

- Where are the border countries of the United States? All of the countries of the world and the states of the United States are shown on the maps illustrated in the Atlas, beginning on page 99.

- What are continents? How many are there? What are they called? Continents are defined and identified on page 31.

What is the *Everything You Need to Know About…Homework* series?

The *Everything You Need to Know About…Homework* series is a set of unique reference resources written especially to answer the homework questions of fourth-, fifth-, and sixth-graders. The series provides information to answer commonly asked homework questions in a variety of subjects. Here you'll find facts, charts, definitions, and explanations, complete with examples and illustrations that will supplement schoolwork colorfully, clearly, and comprehensively.

A Note to Parents

It's important to support your children's efforts to do homework. Welcome their questions and see that they have access to a well-lighted desk or table, pencils, paper, and any other books or equipment that they need—such as rulers, calculators, reference books or textbooks, and so on. You might also set aside a special time each day for doing homework, a time when you're available to answer questions that may arise. But don't do your child's homework for them. Remember, homework should create a bond between school and home. It is meant to enhance the lessons taught at school on a daily basis, and to promote good work and study habits. Although it is gratifying to have your children present flawless homework papers, the flawlessness should be a result of your children's explorations and efforts—not your own.

The *Everything You Need to Know About…Homework* series is designed to help your children complete their homework on their own to the best of their abilities. If they're stuck, you can use these books with them to help find answers to troubling homework problems. And remember, when the work is done, praise your children for a job well done.

Chapter 1 Geography Defined

What Is Geography?

Geography is the study of the world, how it works, and how people use and change the world as they live in it. The word **geography** comes from the Greek words **geo**, meaning "earth," and **graph**, meaning "writing."

GEOGRAPHY EXPLORES MANY IMPORTANT QUESTIONS ABOUT WHERE AND HOW WE LIVE, INCLUDING:

1 What is the earth like?

2 Where are things located on the earth?

3 Who lives where on the earth?

4 Why is one place different from another?

5 How do people and places influence one another?

A *geographer* is a person who studies geography. A professional geographer is a person who studies or teaches geography for a living or who uses geography in his or her job. For example, people who make road atlases or people who decide where new toy stores should be built may be geographers.

The Five Themes of Geography

Geographical thinking centers around five basic ideas, or themes.

1 PLACE

When a geographer says "place," he or she is talking about physical and human characteristics. Physical characteristics are the shapes of landforms and bodies of water, climate, soil, and plant and animal life. Human characteristics include the number of people living in a certain place, how close together they live, social traits, cultural traditions, and political institutions.

2 LOCATION

When a geographer says "location," he or she is talking about the importance of where one thing is in relation to another. When you study location, you study how physical characteristics (such as harbors, rivers, fertile plains, and mountainous terrain) affect human settlement and the ways in which places are used.

3 HUMAN AND ENVIRONMENTAL INTERACTION

When a geographer talks about human and environmental interaction, he or she is talking about the changes people have made in their environment and the changes they continue to make.

4 HUMAN MOVEMENT

A geographer who studies human movement follows the routes people take when they move from one place to another and tries to explain why these movements are necessary. He or she also studies the effects this movement has on the areas where people move and settle.

5 REGIONS

A geographer thinking about regions looks at what makes one area different from another. To do that, he or she studies physical and human characteristics to see where they change.

> *Social traits* describe the things people do and say, and how they behave in groups. Social traits are influenced by population (see pp. 58–64) and culture (see pp. 65–74).

Geography and You

You don't need textbooks or classroom teaching to begin learning and using geography. In fact, you use geography every day—probably without realizing it.

MENTAL MAPS AND SKETCHES

Mental maps are maps you picture in your mind.

Close your eyes and imagine the inside of your bedroom. Where is the bed? How do you get from the bed to the bedroom door? Once you're at the door, which way do you go to get to the kitchen? How about from the kitchen to the front door? From your home to your school, playground, park, or grocery store?

If you are able to picture places in relation to one another, you are creating mental maps. Mental maps can be of any place, large or small. You will use mental maps all your life to help you understand where you are compared to other parts of your world.

A rough drawing of a mental map is a *map sketch*. If you draw your mental map on paper or on your computer, for example, you will have made a map sketch.

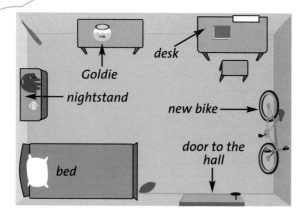

Our first mental maps are usually of our homes.

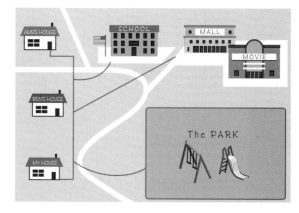

As we grow older, we create new maps to include neighborhoods and parks.

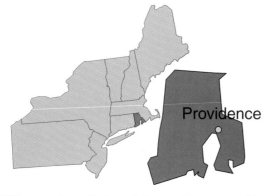

With more knowledge of the world, we are able to locate ourselves in larger areas. For example, we can think of our town within our state, our state within our country, our country within the world.

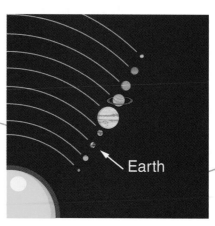

With still more knowledge, we can picture the earth in the solar system, the solar system in the galaxy, and the galaxy in the universe.

The Geography of Geography

Geography is about the "where" of things, so it's an important part of many subjects, including biology, weather sciences, history, and geology. Today, geographers usually study the geography important to one branch of learning. Among the many subfields of geography are:

1. **Agricultural geography,** the study of farming in different parts of the world.

2. **Biogeography,** the study of plants and animals in different geographic locations and climates.

3. **Cartography,** the science of making maps.

4. **Climatology,** the study of world climates.

5. **Cultural geography,** the study of people and their ways of life in different parts of the world.

6. **Geomorphology,** the study and measurement of landforms on the earth's surface and under water.

7. **Historical geography,** the study of how geography affected historical events.

8. **Industrial and marketing geography,** the study of locations for businesses and factories and how particular locations can benefit or hurt them.

9. **Meteorology,** the study of daily weather, including air temperature, precipitation (rainfall, snowfall, etc.), and winds.

10. **Political geography,** the study of nations and states, including the natural habitats, cities, farms, and populations within them.

11. **Resource geography,** the study of the location of natural resources and the conservation of those resources to meet human needs.

12. **Urban geography,** the study of how cities develop and work.

Galactic Address

A good first step toward making a mental map of yourself within the universe is to write your galactic address.

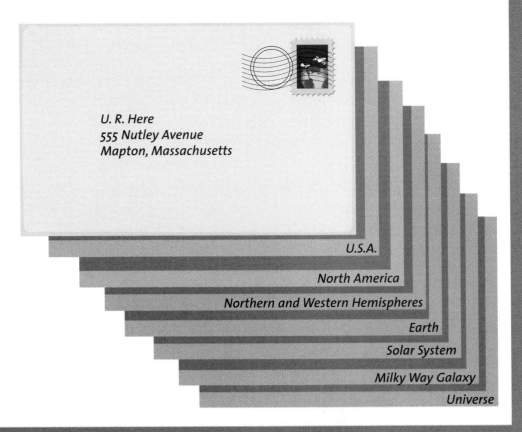

U. R. Here
555 Nutley Avenue
Mapton, Massachusetts

U.S.A.

North America

Northern and Western Hemispheres

Earth

Solar System

Milky Way Galaxy

Universe

Geographical Thinking

Picture yourself in Antarctica. What do you see? What are you wearing?

Now picture yourself near the equator. Now what do you see? Are you wearing a parka and snow pants?

You probably already know many geographical words and phrases that produce clear mental pictures. When you think of the word "cold," for example, do you think of "north," "south," "east," or "west"? If you live in North America, which direction makes you think of "hot"? What do you picture when you think "mountain," "valley," "city," or "swamp"?

Geographical thinking is the ability to think about places and their characteristics. If Antarctica makes you think of a cold place or the equator of a hot one, you are thinking geographically.

Geographical thinking helps you select the appropriate clothes for climate and weather conditions, among other things.

The First Geographers

The first geographers were people who, like you, made mental maps and thought about things geographically. However, they didn't stop there. They traveled around, remembered what they saw, and recorded their experiences so other people could learn from them.

Early humans who followed animal migrations in order to hunt for food might be considered the first geographers. So, too, might those people who left their homelands to explore unknown areas and, later, returned to tell of their discoveries.

Thales: The First True Geographer?

Thales (c. 640–550 B.C.) was a man who lived on the shores of the Aegean Sea in Greece more than 2,500 years ago. He established methods for observing places. Thales traveled widely. He journeyed to markets far from his home to trade goods. Along the way, he wrote down all the new things he saw and learned. He also described a way to measure the distances and directions that set one place apart from another. His method was much like the systems of miles and kilometers we use to measure distances today. His information helped later geographers make accurate globes and maps (see p. 12). Because Thales was so careful about his observations, many scholars consider him one of the first true geographers.

The ancient Greeks were the first people to make a specific list of things to observe about places, such as the distance from other places or landmarks, the number of people in the place, the number of buildings, the sources of water, etc. Because of their attention to detail and careful descriptions, they are considered the first real geographers. The Greeks were also the first people to develop the theory that Earth is round, a theory proved to be true hundreds of years later.

Representing the Earth: Globes, Projections, and Maps

Globes

Looking at Earth

A map of the solar system shows Earth in relation to the Sun and the other planets.

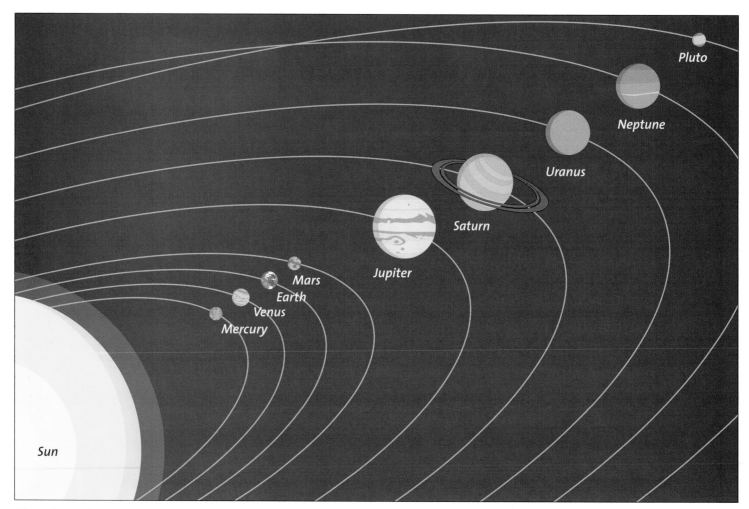

The solar system

This photograph of the earth from outer space shows water and land formations, as well as cloud cover.

Like the other planets, Earth is shaped like a sphere. From outer space, it looks like a disk covered by clouds.

But a photograph can show only half the earth—or one **hemisphere** (see p. 10). To show the whole earth, we use a **globe**, or a sphere-shaped model of the earth. Although it doesn't show all the cloud formations and wind patterns in the atmosphere, it does show the land and water formations on the earth's surface. Globes also help us understand natural events, among them day and night and the seasons.

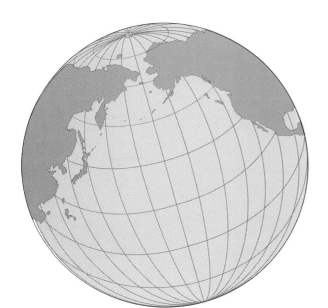

Globes show the water and land formations on the earth's surface.

Inventing the Globe

You can tell by photographs taken from space that the earth is round. But, if you look out a window at school or home, the surface of the earth appears mainly flat.

Yet more than 2,000 years before photography from space was possible, the ancient Greek geographers relied on observation and mathematics to figure out the shape and size of the earth. They made the first globes to show what the earth is shaped like.

Lines of Longitude and Latitude

The ancient Greeks also used their globes to think about the location of places on the earth. They divided the globe into 360 segments, called **degrees**. They used vertical **lines of longitude** to mark off the 360 parts. Longitude lines, also called **meridians**, are still used today to locate places on the earth, and to measure the distances between places. They can be seen on most globes.

The **prime meridian**, or 0 degrees (0°) longitude, was agreed upon in 1884. It passes through the site of the Royal Naval Observatory in Greenwich, England. Distance is measured east and west of this line. Longitude lines east of the prime meridian are numbered 1° through 179°. This is the **eastern hemisphere**. Longitude lines west of the prime meridian are also numbered 1° through 179°. This is the **western hemisphere**. The 180° line, reached by traveling east or west from the prime meridian, is exactly halfway around the earth from the prime meridian. Much of this line of longitude is also used as the **international date line** (see p. 15).

The ancient Greeks also drew lines to divide the earth horizontally. These lines are called **lines of latitude** or **parallels**. Latitude is measured from the **equator**, or 0 degrees (0°) latitude. Latitude lines are numbered from 0° to 90° from the equator to the north pole. The part of the earth from the equator to the north pole is called the **northern hemisphere**. Latitude lines are also numbered 0° to 90° from the equator to the south pole. The part of the earth from the equator to the south pole is called the **southern hemisphere**.

The northern hemisphere is divided into the tropics and the temperate zone at the Tropic of Cancer, a line of latitude that runs parallel to the equator at 23°30′ north latitude. The temperate zone runs from 23°30′ to the Arctic Circle, a line of latitude located at 66°30′ north latitude. In the southern hemisphere, the Tropic of Capricorn, located at 23°30′ south latitude, divides the tropics from the southern temperate zone. The temperate zone ends at the Antarctic Circle, or 66°30′ south latitude.

Lines of latitude run parallel to each other; that means they never meet.

Degrees of longitude and latitude are divided into measures called *minutes*, and marked by the symbol ′. Like minutes in an hour, there are 60 minutes (60′) in a degree of longitude or latitude. Minutes are divided into seconds, and marked by the symbol ″. There are 60 seconds in each minute of latitude or longitude.

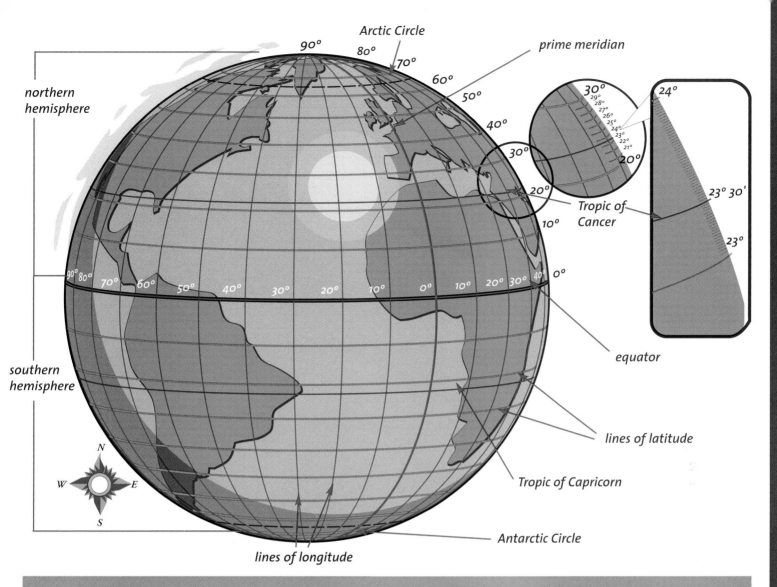

northern
hemisphere

90° 80° 70° 60° 50° 40° 30° 20° 10° 0°

Arctic Circle

prime meridian

30°
29°
28°
27°
26°
25°
24°
23°
22°
21°
20°

24°

23° 30'

23°

Tropic of
Cancer

equator

90° 80° 70° 60° 50° 40° 30° 20° 10° 0° 10° 20° 30° 40°

southern
hemisphere

lines of latitude

Tropic of Capricorn

N
W   E
S

Antarctic Circle

lines of longitude

The Two North Poles

The spot where the lines of longitude meet at the
northernmost point of the globe is called the **north
pole**. It is also called **true north**, or **geographic
north**.

There is another north pole, called **magnetic
north**. The magnetic north pole is not located in
quite the same place as the geographical north
pole, although they are very close. The difference
between the location of the true north and
magnetic north poles is shown on most globes.

You can find the magnetic north pole with a
compass. A compass is made of a magnetized
needle held up so that it turns freely. Because the
earth itself is a huge magnet, no matter what
direction you're going, the compass needle
always points to magnetic north.

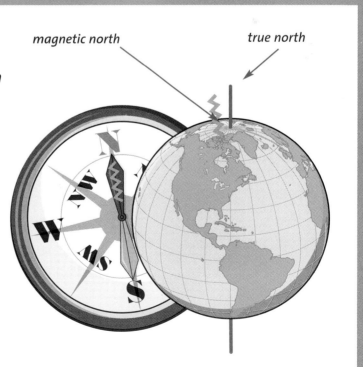

magnetic north

true north

Geographers in Ancient Greece

Greek geographers established the science of making highly accurate globes. The globes are based on some of the most important discoveries made by early Greek geographers.

Eratosthenes of Cyrene (c. 280–200 B.C.) used math and his knowledge of round objects (spheres), to measure the circumference of the earth. His measurement was close to the measurement used by scientists today (24,902 miles; 40,075 kilometers).

Hipparchus (born c. 150 B.C.) refined measurements for **latitude** and developed measures for **longitude** (see p. 10). He was the first to divide the equator into 360 degrees. Hipparchus also divided the world as he knew it into climatic zones (see p. 50) and drew the first known map of the night sky.

Strabo (60 B.C.–A.D. 25) described his travels through Europe, North Africa, and western Asia in a work called **Geographia**. Written as 17 volumes, *Geographia* describes in detail the world as the Greeks of his time knew it.

Claudius Ptolemy (2nd century A.D.) wrote an eight-volume book, also called **Geographia**. In it, he described in terms of longitude and latitude (see p. 10) all the places in the world that were known to the Greeks of this time.

The Geographic Grid

Lines of latitude and longitude form a **geographic grid**.

The geographic grid makes it possible to identify points on the earth and record their exact locations north or south of the equator and east or west of the prime meridian.

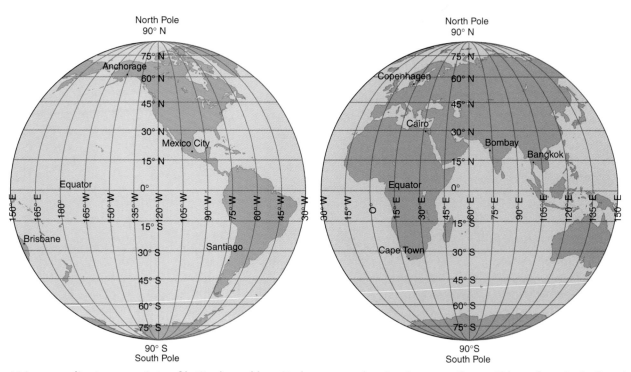

Using coordinates, or points of latitude and longitude, you can locate places on the earth's surface, including Anchorage, Alaska (61° north latitude, 150° west longitude), Bangkok, Thailand (14° north latitude, 100° east longitude), Bombay, India (19° north latitude, 73° east longitude), Brisbane, Australia (27° south latitude, 153° east longitude), Cairo, Egypt (30° north latitude, 31° east longitude), Cape Town, South Africa (34° south latitude, 18° east longitude), Copenhagen, Denmark, (56° north latitude, 12° east longitude), Mexico City, Mexico (19° north latitude, 99° west longitude), and Santiago, Chile (33° south latitude, 71° west longitude).

Light on Earth

Light on earth is a result of our planet's position in relation to the sun and moon. Our position in space results in such events as day and night, the seasons, solstices, eclipses, and tides.

DAY AND NIGHT

A globe and a lightbulb illustrate how day changes into night. Only half the surface of the globe is covered in light at any time.

As the globe rotates on its axis, the part of the surface that is lighted changes.

Just like the globe in the example, the earth rotates on an axis. As a particular place on the earth rotates out of the sunlight, night falls. As that place rotates back into the light, day dawns.

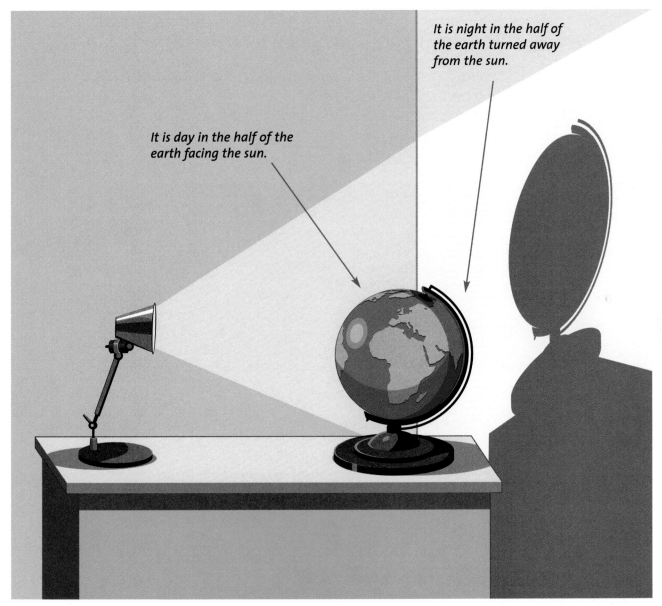

It is night in the half of the earth turned away from the sun.

It is day in the half of the earth facing the sun.

A lightbulb shining on a globe shows how the earth is lit by the sun. Half of the surface is covered by light, the other half is in shadow. As the earth rotates on its axis, every point on the earth moves from the light, or day, to shadow, night, and back again.

THE SEASONS

A globe and a lightbulb can also illustrate how the seasons change. Earth not only rotates on its axis, it also orbits the sun. The angle of the axis is tilted in relation to its orbit. When the earth is positioned so that the northern hemisphere is tipped toward the sun, it is summer there and winter in the southern hemisphere.

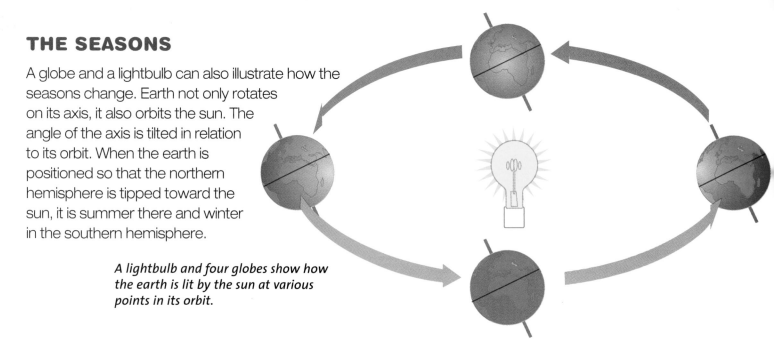

A lightbulb and four globes show how the earth is lit by the sun at various points in its orbit.

ECLIPSES

Occasionally the light from the sun or the sunlight reflected off the moon is kept from hitting the earth, or **eclipsed**, by the position of the earth and moon in relation to the sun.

A **solar eclipse** occurs when the moon passes between the earth and the sun. People standing in the shadow see the moon pass in front of the sun, blotting out its light.

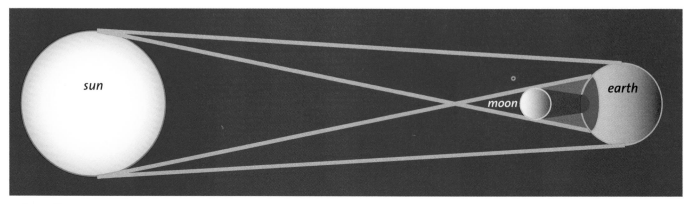

solar eclipse

A **lunar eclipse** occurs when the earth passes between the sun and the moon. People on the side of the earth facing the moon see the moon pass from sunlight into the shadow cast by the earth.

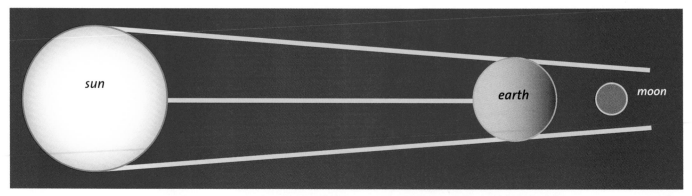

lunar eclipse

The 24-Hour Globe: Time Zones

In addition to lines of longitude and latitude, the globe is marked off into 24 **time zones**. The time zones run in the same direction as the lines of longitude, and begin at 0 degrees (0°), or the **prime meridian**. The time zone that lines up roughly along 180° longitude follows the **international date line**. Places to the east of this line are a calendar day behind places to the west. If you fly from west to east over the international date line on Saturday, you fly into Friday. You gain one day on your trip.

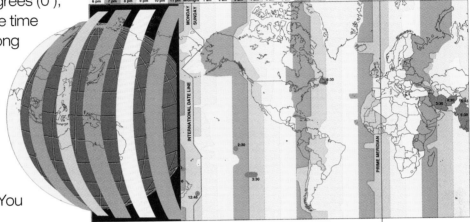

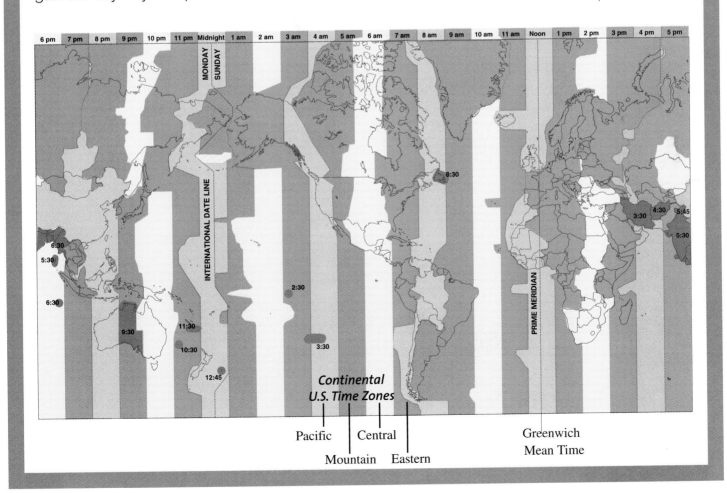

Continental
U.S. Time Zones

Pacific   Central   Greenwich
                               Mean Time
      Mountain   Eastern

2 Maps

What Is a Map?

A *map* is a picture of a place on a flat surface. Most maps show a place drawn from above.

Different types of maps show different types of information, such as natural features, where humans live, historical and modern political boundaries, centers of industry, and variations in climate and weather.

Map Projections

Imagine peeling the surface off a globe and laying it down flat. It would form a map with a very unusual shape.

Globes accurately show sizes, locations, and distances on the earth because the earth, like a globe, is roughly a sphere. Because they are flat, maps do not show the round earth exactly as it is shown on a globe.

In order to make maps, mapmakers use *projections* based on the geographical grid (see p. 12). In order to take the grid from a globe and open it flat on a map, the grid must be changed somewhat. These changes affect the accuracy of maps.

Standard map projections are created to represent the geographic grid as accurately as possible on flat surfaces. In inventing projections, mapmakers have four major concerns: area, direction, distance, and shape.

When mapmakers make projections, they must decide which elements need to be most accurate on their maps. If a map is going to be used to measure the distance between places, a mapmaker will choose a projection that shows the size of land and water areas as accurately as possible to scale. If a mapmaker needs to show direction and the shape of the land and water areas, he or she will choose a projection that depicts those features most accurately.

MAPMAKERS' CONCERNS

area	The size of land and water regions in relation to each other.
direction	North, south, east, and west compared with their true locations on the geographic grid.
distance	The distance between locations on a map relative to the earth's surface, called scale.
shape	The shapes of land and water areas compared with their shapes on the earth or a globe.

Some Common Map Projections

Conic

Used for mapping a large piece of the earth's surface, it shows accurate distance, direction, and shape for the limited area mapped.

Interrupted
(equal area)

Shows accurate area and shape. Oceans have open, pie-shaped interruptions to adjust for distance.

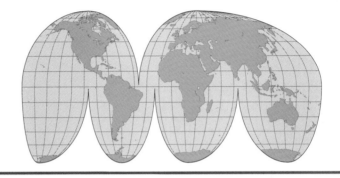

Mercator
(cylindrical)

Shows accurate direction, but land and water areas are greatly distorted toward the north and south poles.

Polar
(azimuthal)

Used for mapping hemispheres instead of the whole earth; shows accurate distance and direction, but shape and size become more and more distorted toward the edges.

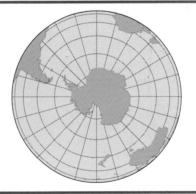

Robinson
(oval)

Shows accurately the shape and size of continents, but the water areas are expanded to fill the extra space.

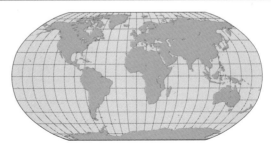

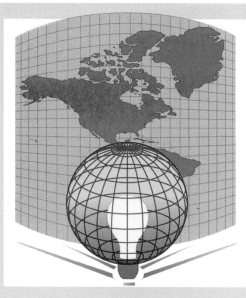

How Map Projections Are Made

Put a projector light inside a globe. The spaces formed by the geographic grid when **projected** from the globe onto a flat screen will change as the projector light is moved. While the location of a city is likely to fall in the same place on the globe and its projection, the sizes and shapes of countries and continents will change as the distances away from the center of the projected image change. Areas on the edges of the map appear stretched as they are flattened in the projection.

When cartographers make maps, they use mathematical calculations to project the geographic grid (see p. 12) onto paper.

Natural Features

Natural features are features on the earth's surface that were not made by humans. These features include nonliving things (rocks, minerals, soil, water, and atmosphere) as well as living things (plants and animals).

PHYSICAL FEATURES

Earth's nonliving, or **physical**, features include mountains, plains, rivers, lakes, and oceans. The earth's physical features are constantly changing. A number of forces, such as erosion and weathering, gradually wear down the earth's surface. Other forces, such as fire, earthquakes, and volcanoes, make almost instant changes (see pp. 32–33).

ATMOSPHERIC FEATURES

The earth's nonliving features also include **atmospheric** conditions, or climate and weather. Climate is the usual weather in a place over a long time period. It, along with physical features, determines which plants and animals can live in a particular place (see pp. 43–49).

LIVING FEATURES

Earth's living features are its plants and animals, including humans. Different plants and animals thrive in different natural regions, or **biomes** (see pp. 50–56). Biomes are large environments that share the same general temperature and annual rainfall.

Human-made Features

Human-made features are features on the earth's surface created by human beings—for example, buildings, monuments, parks, roads, fields, and landfills.

> *Cartography* is the art of making maps or charts. People who draw maps are called *cartographers*. The words come from the Latin *carta*, meaning "map," and the Greek *graph*, meaning "writing."

The First Maps

No one knows for certain who made the first maps or what those maps looked like. But we know that humans have been making maps for thousands of years. Scratched into sand, painted on animal skins, carved into wood, or drawn on rock walls, maps helped people avoid danger, find good hunting grounds, and locate clean water. The ancient Egyptians even supplied maps to tax collectors to help them along their routes.

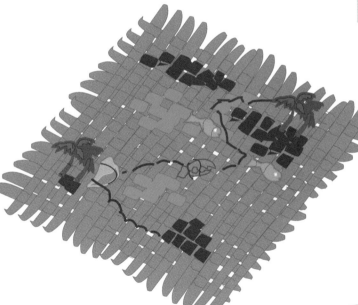

More than 2,000 years ago, Europeans were drawing maps to help them navigate at sea. Called **charts**, these maps of waterways were drawn on skins and stones, carved in wood, or engraved into clay—in much the same way as land maps were made. Pacific islanders made charts out of palm leaves woven through reeds. The pattern of the weaving showed ocean currents and wave directions. Shells were attached to the reed charts to show where islands were located.

The oldest maps that exist today were made in the ancient Middle Eastern civilization of Babylon. These maps are more than 4,000 years old, and are etched into large clay tablets.

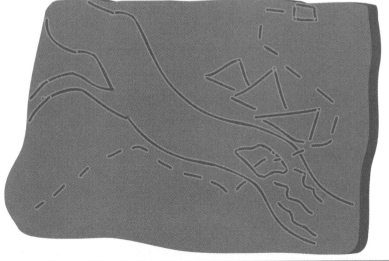

Three Basic Kinds of Maps

POLITICAL MAPS

Political maps show how humans have divided up the earth's surface. They show borders between countries, the locations of cities and towns, building sites, neighborhoods, settlement plans, roadways, and other human-made features.

Geopolitical maps show political and physical features on one map. (See p. 28 for an example of a geopolitical map.)

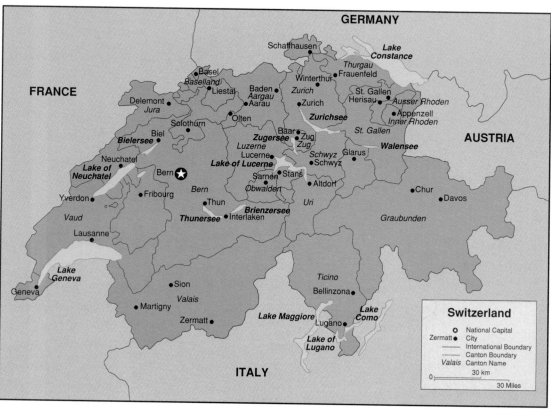

This political map of Switzerland shows the countries it borders, as well as its cantons (states) and major cities.

PHYSICAL MAPS

Physical maps show the land formations and water on the earth's surface. Physical maps show mountains, valleys, plains, oceans, rivers, and lakes. They can also show locations of natural plant life, water currents, and wind patterns.

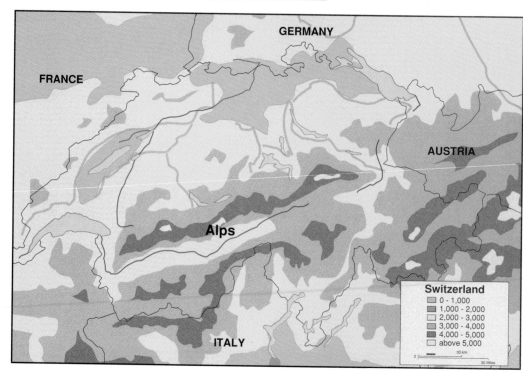

This physical map of Switzerland shows variations in the elevation of the land, as well as the locations of major rivers.

20

CULTURAL MAPS

Cultural maps show such patterns as ethnic groups, religious practices, languages spoken, customs, educational levels, and recreational choices.

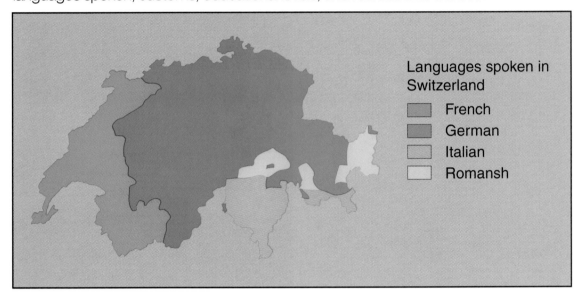

This cultural map of Switzerland shows where different languages are spoken within the country.

Charts

Charts are maps of bodies of water. Sailors use them to navigate in open ocean waters as well as on lakes and in shallow bays, inlets, and rivers. Charts show water depths, currents, and physical features found below the surface of the water. They also locate ports and places to anchor safely, as well as buoys, lighthouses, and other aids to seafarers.

The depth of water is shown in feet on this sample chart.

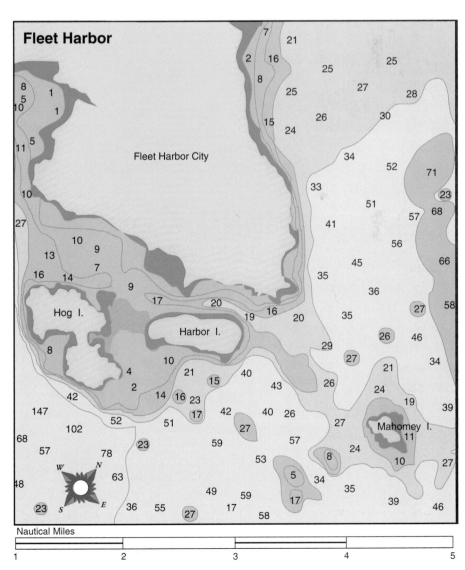

Maps for Special Uses

RELATIVE LOCATION MAPS

Relative location maps show the position of a place in relation to its surroundings. For example, such a map might show where a specific place is located in relation to the rest of the world.

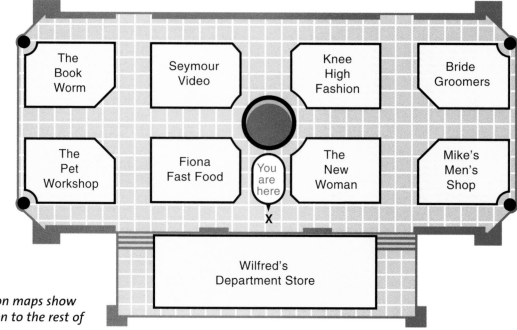

In shopping malls, relative location maps show where you are standing in relation to the rest of the mall and its stores.

DISTRIBUTION MAPS

Distribution maps show how things are spread out across an area or throughout the world. For example, distribution maps may show where sheep are raised on all the continents or where oil wells are located in Oklahoma. Distribution maps can also show where rain forests and timber mills are located, what kinds of rocks make up the earth's surface, or where bookstores are located in your hometown.

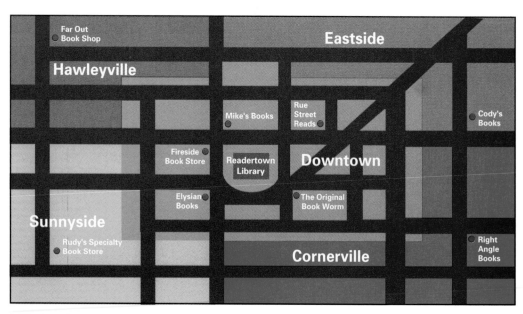

This distribution map shows the location of bookstores in Readertown. According to the map, most bookstores are downtown, and the rest of Readertown's bookstores are evenly distributed in the residential neighborhoods.

TOPOGRAPHIC MAPS

Topographic maps show physical features, and are often drawn showing **contours**, or lines that show differences in elevation. Any topographic map drawn to show contours may also be called a **contour map**.

This section of a topographic map shows color-keyed contours, as well as a variety of physical features: roads, railroad tracks, bridges, and an air strip.

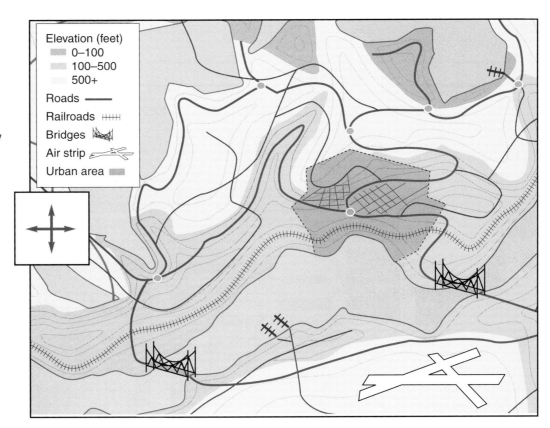

CLIMATE AND WEATHER MAPS

Climate and **weather maps** show how and where climatic and weather conditions occur across a region or throughout the world.

Weather map illustrating a fall day in the United States

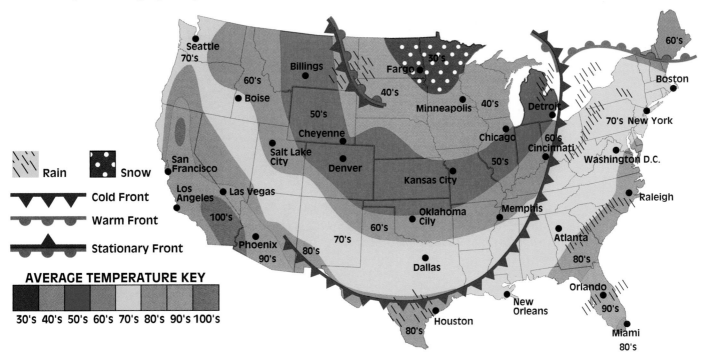

TIME ZONE MAPS

Time zone maps show how the earth is divided into different time zones.
(See p. 15 for an example of a time zone map.)

ALTERED STATES: Cartograms

Cartograms are diagrams in map form. The places on a cartogram are drawn in mathematical proportion to show how much of a particular thing is found in each mapped area.

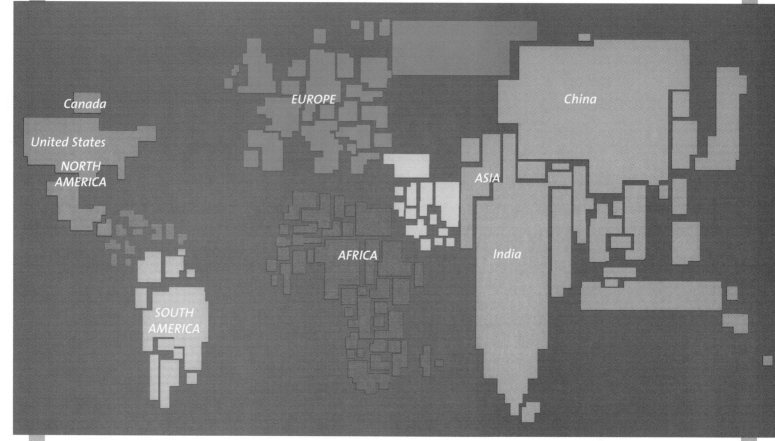

Drawn from data collected from the U.S. Bureau of the Census International Database

A cartogram of world population shows China and India as much larger than North American and European countries. Anyone looking at this cartogram can tell at a glance that there are more people in China than in the United States and Canada combined.

Written References:
Geographical Dictionaries and Almanacs

Maps and globes are the most important tools you will need to do your geography homework, but **geographical dictionaries** and **almanacs** are very useful, too.

Hoth·am, Mount \-'häth-əm\. Mountain in the Darg Plateau, E Victoria, SE Australia, SW of Mt. Kosciusko; 6108 ft.

Ho–t'ien \'hō-'tyen\ *also* Kho·tan \'kō-'tän\. 1 River, W Sinkiang Uighur, W China; joins the Yarkand to form Tarim river, but dry much of the year.
2 Town, China. See KHOTAN 2.

Hotin. See KHOTIN.

Hot Spring. County in Arkansas. See table at ARKANSAS.

Hot Springs. 1 County in Wyoming. See table at WYOMING.
2 City, ⊗ of Garland co., W cen. Arkansas, in Ouachita Mts. 47 m. WSW of Little Rock; pop. (1970c) 35,631; health and tourist resort noted for its 47 thermal springs. Settled 1807; made, with surrounding area, a U.S. Government reservation 1832, Hot Springs National Park 1921 (see UNITED STATES, *National Parks*).
3 City, New Mexico. See TRUTH OR CONSEQUENCES.
4 City, ⊗ of Fall River co., SW corner of South Dakota, in foothills of Black Hills 48 m. S of Rapid City; pop. (1970c) 4434; health resort; thermal and mineral springs; sandstone quarries; mica, feldspar, gold, silver mines.
5 Village, Bath co., W Virginia, 5 m. SW of Warm Springs; mineral springs; Japanese diplomats interned here 1942 at beginning of war with Japan; scene of United Nations Conference on Food and Agriculture 1943.

Hot Springs Peak. Mountain, Humboldt co., NW Nevada; 6450 ft.

Hot Sul·phur Springs \-'səl-fər-\. Town, ⊗ of Grand co., N Colorado; pop. (1970c) 220; hot sulfur springs.

Hotte, Massif de la. See SUD, MASSIF DU.

Hot·ten·tot Point \ˌhät-ᵊn-ˌtät-\. Cape on SW coast of South-West Africa, N of Lüderitz.

Hou·dain \ü-'daⁿ\. Commune, Pas-de-Calais dept., N France, near Béthune; pop. (1962c) 8869; coal; has church (12th and 16th cents.); destroyed in World War I and rebuilt.

Hou·dan \ü-'däⁿ\. Village, Yvelines dept., N France; pop. (1962c) 2358; has 15th–16th cent. church and keep of an early 12th cent. castle; noted for its poultry market, the Houdan breed of domestic fowl originating here.

Hou·deng–Goe·gnies \ü-ˌdäⁿ-gər-'nyē\. Commune, Hainaut prov., SW Belgium, on a tributary of the Haine, E of Mons; pop. (1969e) 8947; coal mines, smelting, woodworking, rope making, glassworks.

Houf·fa·lize \ˌü-fə-'lēz\. Village, Luxembourg prov., SE Belgium, 10 m. N of Bastogne; pop. (1969e) 1346; taken by Germans in ~ly phase ~ le of the Bulge Dec. 1944;

Geographical dictionaries, or gazetteers, *are made up of alphabetical lists of geographic names. General gazetteers list all kinds of geographical features—including countries, cities, counties, landforms, bodies of water, and more—each followed by a brief description. The description usually tells the size and location of a feature, as well as how to pronounce its name. Gazetteers often define the location of a place by latitude and longitude coordinates, or by the number of miles it is from a well-known location.*

Almanacs, unlike geographical dictionaries, are not organized alphabetically. Instead, they have detailed indexes to help you locate geographic information.

New Jersey
(see States, U.S.)
Admission, area, capital......386,640
Agriculture.............160,161,162,163
Altitudes (high, low)....................385
Birth, death statistics.................939
Bridges............................622-624
Budget.......................................154
Chamber of Commerce.............640
Commerce at ports 674
Congressmen.................74,579,583
Courts, U.S. 596
Debt...154
Ethnic, racial distribution............640
Fair..640
Geographic center 387
Governors 598,601
Income, per capita 640
Interest, laws, rates...................713
Marriages, divorce laws722-723,942
Name, origin of..........................388
Population 129

Parts of a Map

Elevation means the height of land above sea level. It is shown on maps using contour lines. Elevation can also be shown using shading or colors.

The *directional arrow* shows the directions—north, south, east, and west, and sometimes northwest, northeast, southeast, and southwest—in relation to the map. These directions show the orientation of the map. Most world maps show north on the top and south on the bottom, east to the right, and west to the left. Maps of smaller areas often use this standard orientation, too. Some directional arrows are plain and simple. Others are decorated.

A *compass rose* is an ornamental directional arrow often used on ship charts and old-fashioned maps. The rose is usually drawn from a circle divided into 360 degrees, and is used to tell directions from magnetic north, or 0 degrees (0°) on the compass.

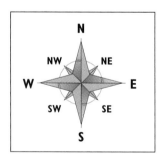

A *map index* is included on some maps. It is a list of place names, complete with coordinates for finding the places on the map.

Symbols, or *icons*, are used on maps to represent real objects or places. Symbols can be simple dots to indicate cities, pictographs (tiny pictures) to indicate products, or colors to show location. Symbols are explained in the map key or legend.

Major Cities

Bologna	D-2
Firenza	D-2
Genova	C-2
Milano	C-1
Palermo	E-4
Roma	E-3
Venezia	E-1

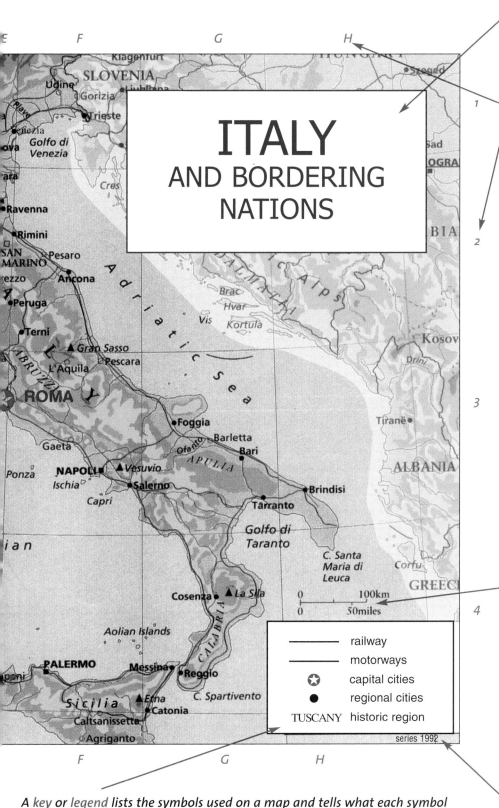

A *title* is included to tell map readers what the map is about.

Coordinates are a set of points or spaces, for example, G-2, located by using the map grid. The map index uses a map grid to help the reader find a specific location.

A *map grid* is a grid drawn on a map. You can read the map grid by looking in the margins of the map. The letters A, B, C, etc., run along the top and bottom margins. The numbers 1, 2, 3, etc., run along the left and right margins. If a place is identified at D-3, simply find the square on the grid where column D and row 3 intersect. The map grid may or may not follow the geographic grid of latitude and longitude. Many highway maps have their own grids.

The map *scale* shows how the size of the map relates to the size of a real place. It may be stated in words, in combinations of words and numbers, and in ratios. For example, if a map's scale is 1 inch=100 miles, one inch on the map represents one hundred miles in the real world.

A *key* or *legend* lists the symbols used on a map and tells what each symbol means. For example, on some maps, cities can be represented by different-sized dots. Large dots can stand for large cities and small dots for small cities or towns. Maps and keys are usually set apart from the rest of a map, often in a box.

Dates appear on many maps to tell when the map was drawn.

Understanding and Comparing Maps

To understand a map, you must be able to "read" it.

Once you can read maps, you can compare maps. By comparing the information on different maps, you can learn how many features work together to make a place special. For example, if you compare a map of North American waterways to a map of North American cities, you'll find that most cities are located on waterways. This is important geographical information—it shows that water is one thing people think about when deciding where to live.

THREE STEPS TO READING MAPS

1 Look at the map *title*. It will tell you what type of information, as well as which region or location, is shown on the map.

2 Look at the map *scale*. Some maps are very simple. Others show a lot of detail. The amount and type of detail on a map depends on the map scale, or the size of the area shown on the map. For example, it would be difficult to show the location of houses on a map of your state. However, it would be a logical feature on a map of your neighborhood. Successfully reading a map means understanding its scale.

3 Look at the *legend*. The legend will tell you what the symbols on the map mean. In order to understand the map fully, you will need to understand the symbols and the type of information they convey.

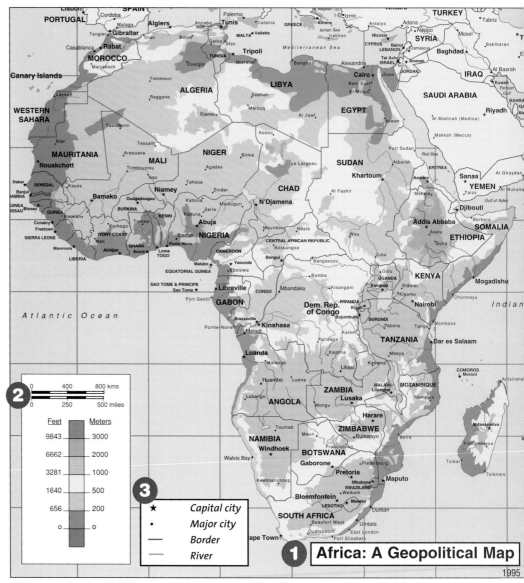

Africa: A Geopolitical Map

1995

Three Steps to Comparing Maps

1 Choose maps that show information you want to compare.

2 Locate your area of interest on both maps.

3 Use the map symbols to read both maps. Then note how the maps are alike and how they are different. When you are using two or more maps, watch for map scale, the type of projections used (see p. 17), and the date the maps were published.

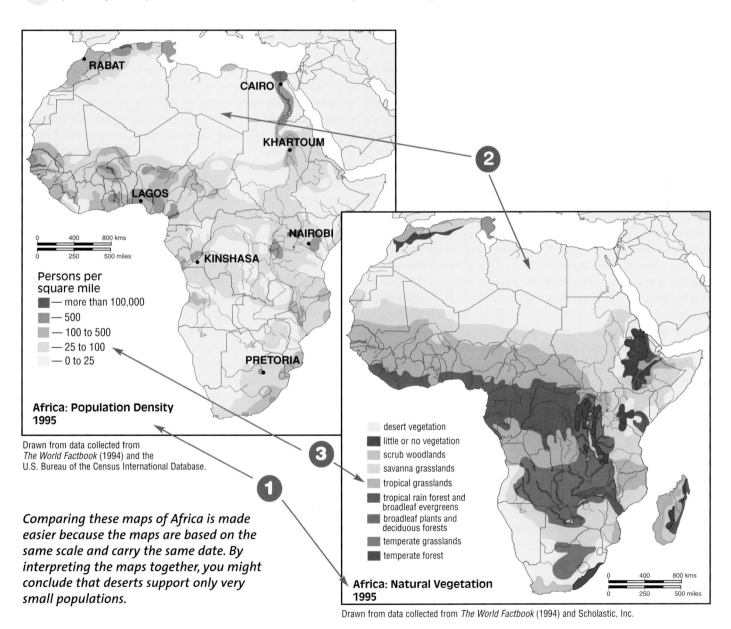

Persons per square mile
- more than 100,000
- 500
- 100 to 500
- 25 to 100
- 0 to 25

Africa: Population Density 1995

Drawn from data collected from *The World Factbook* (1994) and the U.S. Bureau of the Census International Database.

Comparing these maps of Africa is made easier because the maps are based on the same scale and carry the same date. By interpreting the maps together, you might conclude that deserts support only very small populations.

- desert vegetation
- little or no vegetation
- scrub woodlands
- savanna grasslands
- tropical grasslands
- tropical rain forest and broadleaf evergreens
- broadleaf plants and deciduous forests
- temperate grasslands
- temperate forest

Africa: Natural Vegetation 1995

Drawn from data collected from *The World Factbook* (1994) and Scholastic, Inc.

29

The Land

How the Earth Was Formed

Geographers believe that about 4.6 billion years ago a cloud of dust particles came together to form a ball of melted rock. The ball cooled over several million years, forming the earth.

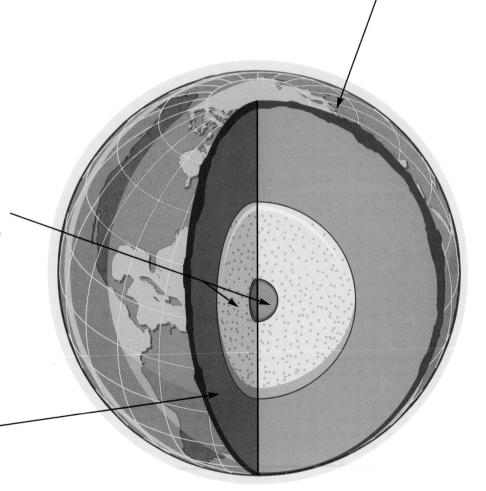

As the molten rock ball cooled, a thin solid layer formed over the surface of the earth. This layer is called the crust. The crust is about 2 miles thick under the deepest parts of the ocean and up to 75 miles thick under the tallest mountain peaks.

The earth's core has two parts: the outer core and the inner core. The outer core is made up of molten rock. The inner core is solid. The core has a radius of about 2,100 miles.

The mantle lies between the earth's crust and core. It is a layer of very hot, sometimes melted rock about 1,800 miles thick.

Plate Tectonics

Continents are the large landmasses on earth: Africa, Australia, Antarctica, North America, South America, and Eurasia. Eurasia is sometimes considered two continents, divided by the Ural Mountains and the Caspian Sea into Europe to the west and Asia to the east.

The crust of the earth is not one solid piece. It is broken into large pieces, called ***tectonic plates***. The plates are like enormous ships that float upon the earth's mantle.

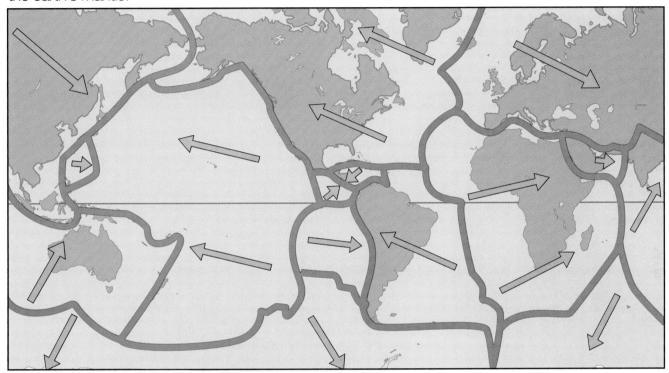

World map showing fault lines and the direction of tectonic plate movement.

FAULT LINES

Fault lines occur along the edges between tectonic plates. As the plates move, a number of tectonic events occur along the fault lines.

PANGAEA AND CONTINENTAL DRIFT

Scientists believe that about 200 million years ago, all the continents were connected. They formed a supercontinent that scientists call ***Pangaea***.

Then the continents separated at places where the tectonic plates broke apart. Like ships on water, the plates slowly moved apart, and the continents we know today were formed.

The continents are still moving. This movement is called ***continental drift***. In another 200 million years, the continents may be connected again or may drift into a completely different arrangement on the planet.

Tectonic Events That Shape the Land

Tectonic plates are moving in different directions at different speeds. The features on the surface of the earth tell us where the plates push beneath each other or collide.

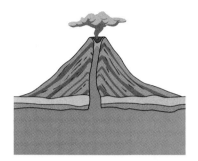

Most *volcanoes* form when molten rock from deep inside the earth rises to the surface at or near a fault line or a soft spot in a plate. The molten rock spurts out of the top of the volcano in the form of lava.

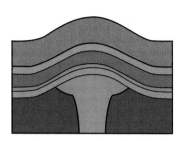

Dome mountains form when molten rock pushes up toward the earth's surface along a fault line but doesn't break through the surface of the earth.

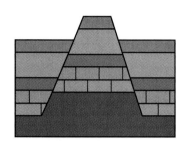

Block mountains form when blocks of rock split along fault lines and slide in opposite directions.

Fold mountains form when tectonic plates move against each other and push and squeeze up the crust of the earth.

VOLCANOES

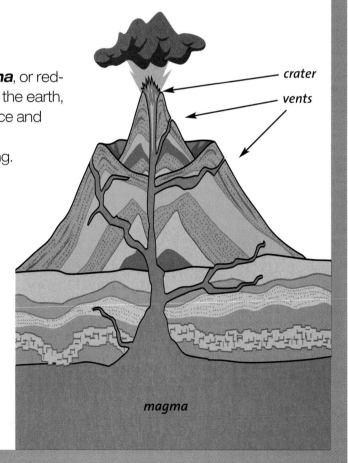

Volcanoes are mountains formed when the **magma**, or red-hot liquid rock and gases that lie below the surface of the earth, rises through vents and passages in the earth's surface and comes out as lava.

Not all volcanoes are **active**, or capable of erupting. In fact, scientists describe four types of volcanoes:

active — erupting constantly

intermittent — erupting at regular intervals

dormant — inactive, but expected to become active again

extinct — inactive for hundreds of years

crater

vents

magma

EARTHQUAKES

Earthquakes are sudden shifting movements in the earth's surface. Some earthquakes cannot even be felt, yet others are strong enough to knock down skyscrapers and twist highways as if they were ribbons. Earthquakes happen when tectonic plates collide, separate, or scrape against one another along fault lines.

1

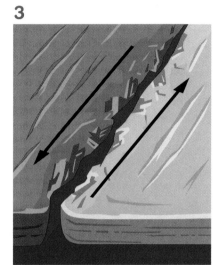

Forces push tectonic plates into one another, causing them to collide or scrape against each other.

2

Over thousands of years, the forces cause the rocks along the fault line to bend and twist.

3

Finally, the force becomes so great that the rocks break loose and jolt past each other, causing an earthquake.

The Ring of Fire
Where Volcanoes and Earthquakes Often Happen

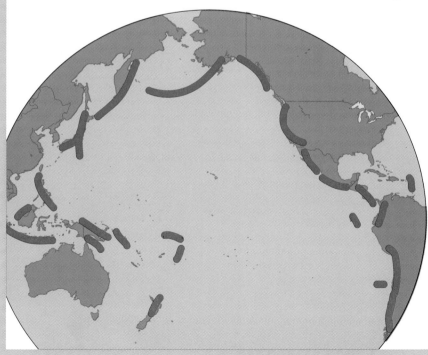

Volcanoes and earthquakes most frequently occur along the fault lines in the earth's tectonic plates. The "ring of fire" in the Pacific Ocean is the world's most active area of earthquake and volcanic activity. Why? The faults in the Atlantic are, for the most part, expanding, or moving away from each other. But in the Pacific, the plates are colliding, or rubbing up against each other (see above, also p. 31).

Landforms

Landforms are the natural features of the earth's land surface, including mountains, other highlands, plains, and lowlands.

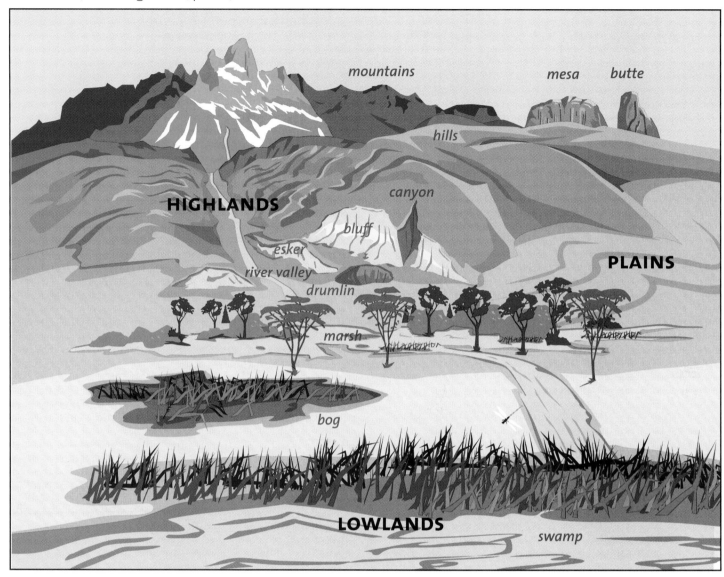

A composite landscape shows many kinds of landforms. (For definitions of the specific landforms, see Glossary, pp. 88–97.)

MOUNTAINS AND HIGHLANDS

A **mountain** is any point on land that rises quickly to at least 1,000 feet above its surroundings. Some mountains are jagged and snowcapped, and others are rounded and smooth. Some are volcanoes, with large craters in their tops.

Mountains exist below the oceans, too. Some of these mountains, while deep under the salty water, rise even higher than Mount Everest, the highest mountain on the continents.

A **hill** is an area on the earth's surface that rises above the land, but not more than 1,000 feet above the surrounding area. Any high land that is not a mountain can be classified as a hill. However, geologists and geographers have developed a special vocabulary for high landforms based on how the landforms were created.

PLAINS

Plains are large, flat, mostly treeless areas of land.

LOWLANDS

A *lowland* is an area of land that is lower than the land surrounding it. Just as geologists and geographers have a special vocabulary for highlands, they have a special vocabulary for lowlands.

A *valley* is a natural low place in the earth's surface, often located between mountains or hills. The bottom of a valley is called its *floor*, the sides its *walls*. A ridge between valleys is called a *divide*. Valleys with steep cliff walls are called *canyons* or *gorges*.

Other natural lowlands are *wetlands*, where the water level stays at or above the land's surface for most of the year. *Bogs*, *marshes*, and *swamps* are the most common types of wetlands.

> **The study of the earth's physical features is called *geomorphology*.**

Erosion and Weathering

Erosion is the gradual wearing away of land by the action of wind, water, or glaciers. **Weathering** is the gradual breakdown of rocks by weather, including wind, rain, snow, and changes in temperature (see p. 44). Erosion and weathering work together constantly to change the landforms on Earth.

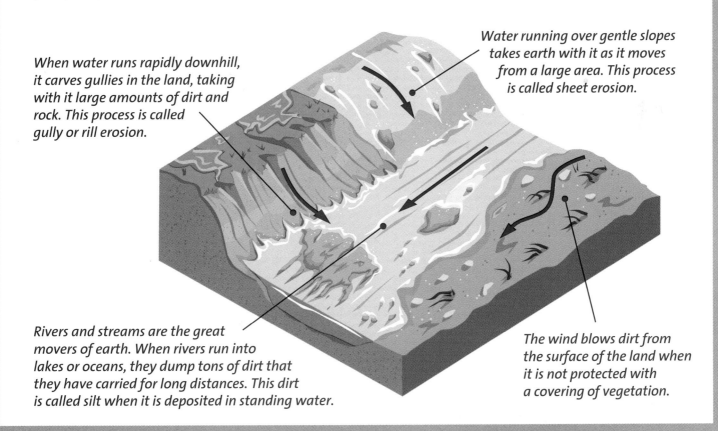

When water runs rapidly downhill, it carves gullies in the land, taking with it large amounts of dirt and rock. This process is called gully or rill erosion.

Water running over gentle slopes takes earth with it as it moves from a large area. This process is called sheet erosion.

Rivers and streams are the great movers of earth. When rivers run into lakes or oceans, they dump tons of dirt that they have carried for long distances. This dirt is called silt when it is deposited in standing water.

The wind blows dirt from the surface of the land when it is not protected with a covering of vegetation.

Glaciers

Glaciers are slow-moving sheets of ice found in high mountain valleys and polar regions. Glaciers cover about six million square miles, or three percent of the earth's surface.

Glaciers form at high latitudes and high elevations, where it is cold enough that more snow falls than melts or evaporates. Over the years, the snow gets deeper and deeper. Pressure from the weight of the snow finally turns the snow into huge sheets of ice. These ice sheets flow, like slow-moving rivers, down mountainsides until they reach warmer air along the oceans or at lower elevations. There the ice sheets melt or break off to form floating **icebergs**.

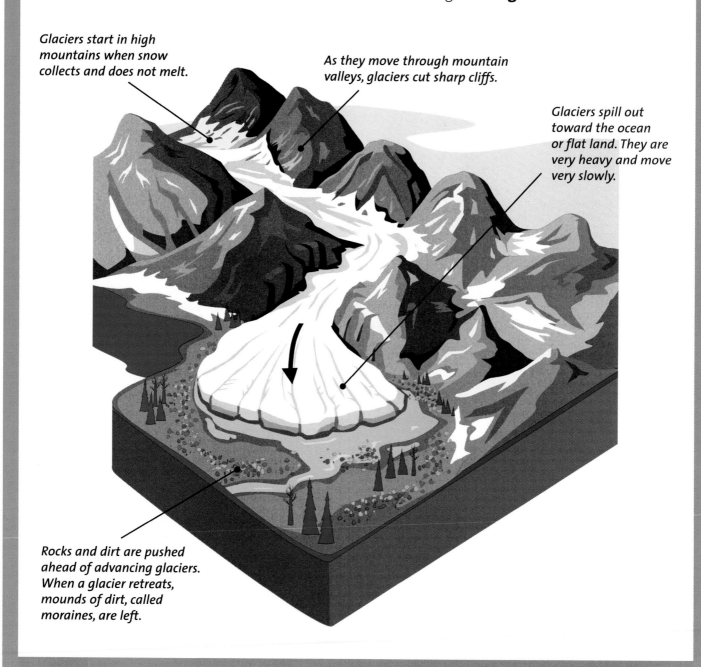

Glaciers start in high mountains when snow collects and does not melt.

As they move through mountain valleys, glaciers cut sharp cliffs.

Glaciers spill out toward the ocean or flat land. They are very heavy and move very slowly.

Rocks and dirt are pushed ahead of advancing glaciers. When a glacier retreats, mounds of dirt, called moraines, are left.

Chapter 2

The Water

Oceans

Oceans are large bodies of salt water that cover almost three-fourths of the earth's surface.

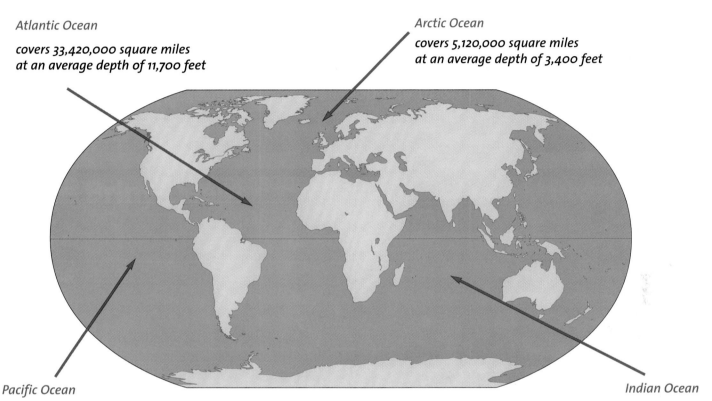

Atlantic Ocean

covers 33,420,000 square miles at an average depth of 11,700 feet

Arctic Ocean

covers 5,120,000 square miles at an average depth of 3,400 feet

Pacific Ocean

covers 64,200,000 square miles at an average depth of 12,900 feet

Indian Ocean

covers 28,400,000 square miles at an average depth of 12,600 feet

The Briny Deep

	Depth (Feet)	Depth (Meters)		Depth (Feet)	Depth (Meters)
Pacific Ocean			**Indian Ocean**		
Mariana Trench	35,800	10,900	**Java Trench**	23,400	7,100
Tonga Trench	35,400	10,800	**Ob' Trench**	22,600	6,900
Philippine Trench	33,000	10,000	**Diamantina Trench**	21,700	6,600
Kermadec Trench	33,000	10,000	**Vema Trench**	21,000	6,400
Atlantic Ocean			**Arctic Ocean**		
Puerto Rico Trench	28,200	8,600	**Eurasia Basin**	17,900	5,500
South Sandwich Trench	27,300	8,300	**Mediterranean Sea**		
Cayman Trench	24,700	7,500	**Ionian Basin**	16,900	5,200
Romanche Gap	24,400	7,400			

The ocean floor, like the surface of the land, is made up of many features. Huge trenches drop off deeply from underwater plains. Plateaus and ridges rise thousands of feet to form mountains on the ocean floor. As on land, the underwater surface is formed by the movements of tectonic plates and shaped by the movement of water (see p. 31 and below).

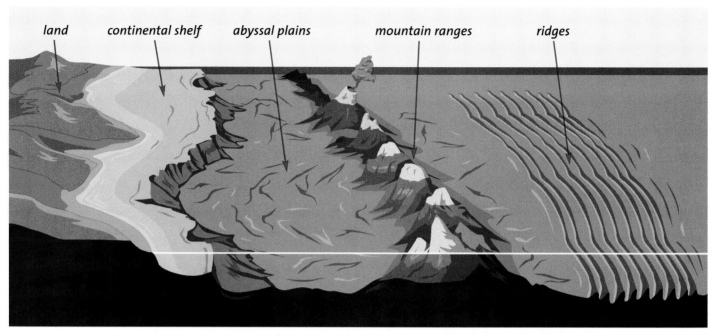

A cross section of the ocean floor shows some of the many features of its landscape.

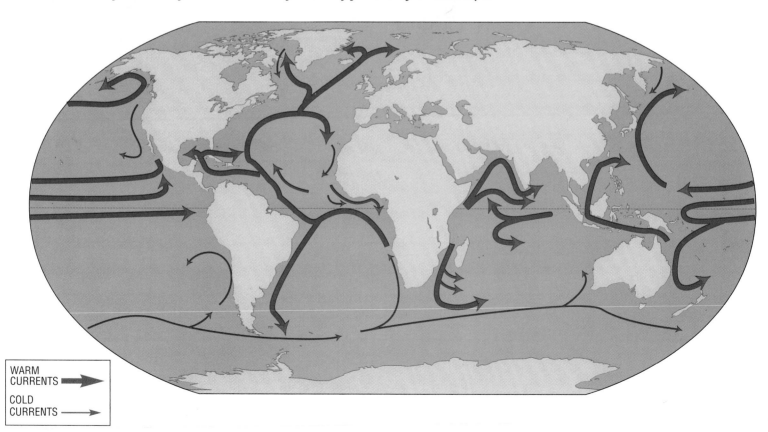

WARM CURRENTS ➡
COLD CURRENTS →

Ocean currents flow in predictable patterns throughout the major water bodies of the earth.

Natural Events Under Water

As on land, erosion, earthquakes, and volcanoes make regular changes under water.

In addition to changing the ocean floor, underwater volcanoes and earthquakes cause giant surges of water in the ocean. These surges of water may range from six to 60 feet high. When the surge of water, called a **tsunami**, hits land, it can cause dangerous flooding and wash away homes, roads, and buildings in its path.

Most tsunamis occur on the coasts of the Pacific Ocean, where volcanic activity occurs regularly.

Tides

Tides are the daily changes in the levels of water in the oceans and seas. They are caused by the gravitational pull of the moon and sun on the earth. The moon affects tides more than the sun does. As the earth rotates on its axis, different parts of the earth face the moon (see pp. 13–14). The energy from gravity moves the water to the part of the ocean nearest the moon, where it piles up, or bulges. Oceans and seas on the opposite side of the earth bulge because of the way the earth spins. The bulges of water travel around the earth from east to west. They bring high tides to the oceans and seashores every 12 hours. When the bulge reaches a shore, it is high tide. When it is away from the shore, it is low tide.

Rivers

Rivers are bodies of water that begin at a source and flow downhill between banks of earth to a **mouth**, where they empty into a larger body of water. Most large rivers have three parts, or **courses**: **upper**, **middle**, and **estuary**.

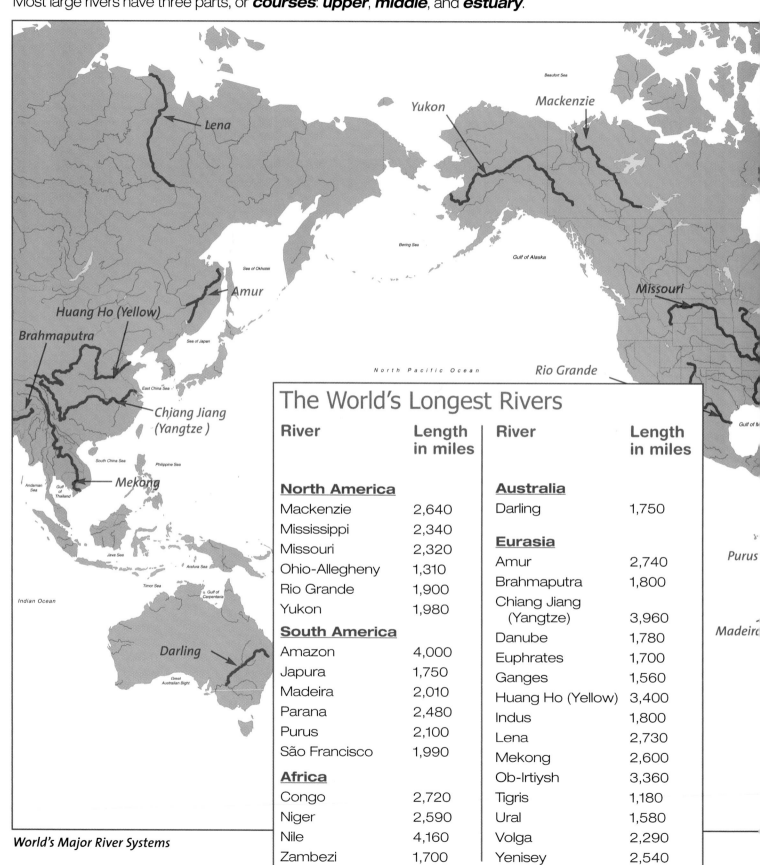

World's Major River Systems

The World's Longest Rivers

River	Length in miles	River	Length in miles
North America		**Australia**	
Mackenzie	2,640	Darling	1,750
Mississippi	2,340		
Missouri	2,320	**Eurasia**	
Ohio-Allegheny	1,310	Amur	2,740
Rio Grande	1,900	Brahmaputra	1,800
Yukon	1,980	Chiang Jiang (Yangtze)	3,960
South America		Danube	1,780
Amazon	4,000	Euphrates	1,700
Japura	1,750	Ganges	1,560
Madeira	2,010	Huang Ho (Yellow)	3,400
Parana	2,480	Indus	1,800
Purus	2,100	Lena	2,730
São Francisco	1,990	Mekong	2,600
Africa		Ob-Irtiysh	3,360
Congo	2,720	Tigris	1,180
Niger	2,590	Ural	1,580
Nile	4,160	Volga	2,290
Zambezi	1,700	Yenisey	2,540

— Ohio-Allegheny

-Mississippi

Greenland Sea

Baffin Bay

Norwegian Sea

Labrador Sea

North Sea

Gulf
of
Bothnia

Baltic Sea

North Atlantic Ocean

English Channel

Bay of Biscay

Tyrrhenian
Sea

Ionian Sea

Mediterranean Sea

Black Sea

Caspian Sea

Aral
Sea

Yenisey

Ob-Irtysh

Volga

Ural

Danube

Tigris

Ganges

Nile

Euphrates

Persian
Gulf

Gulf of Oman

Red
Sea

Arabian Sea

Gulf of Aden

Indus

Bay of Bengal

Amazon

São Francisco

apura

Niger

Congo

Parana

Zambezi

South Atlantic Ocean

Indian Ocean

PARTS OF A RIVER

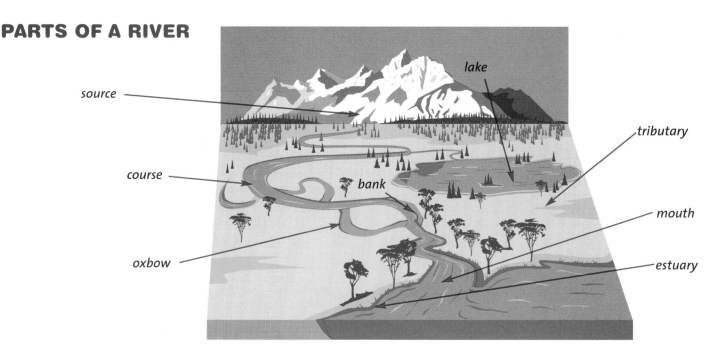

The source of the river shown here is melted water from a glacier, although rivers also form from the waters of highland springs and lakes flowing downhill, and from a combination of these waters. All rivers flow from a source to a mouth, where river waters empty into a larger body of water, sometimes another river, or a bay, gulf, lake, sea, or ocean. (For definitions of specific river parts, see Glossary, pp. 88–97.)

Seas, Gulfs, and Bays

Seas are large bodies of salt water or fresh water that are partly or completely enclosed by land. **Gulfs** and **bays** are large bodies of ocean or sea water that are partly surrounded by land. Bays are usually smaller than gulfs.

Lakes

Lakes are natural and human-made low spots on the land that have filled with water from flooding, melting glacial ice, rivers, and groundwater traveling downhill.

> Most lakes hold fresh water, although some hold salt water.
>
> **Ponds** are small lakes.

FOUR KINDS OF LAKES

Lakes can be divided into four types, depending on how they are formed.

CRATER LAKE

Water collects in craters left by volcanoes.

GLACIAL LAKE

Ice from glaciers carves depressions (low areas) in the landscape. The ice melts and forms a lake.

RIFT VALLEY LAKE

Shifts in plates on the earth's surface form depressions that fill with water.

ARTIFICIAL LAKE

Lakes are created artificially by building dams on rivers or by digging depressions and filling them with water from nearby sources.

The Air: Atmosphere, Weather, and Climate

Chapter 3

The Atmosphere

The **atmosphere** is the air that surrounds the earth. It is made up of five main layers. Although we don't pay much attention to the atmosphere most of the time, it is taller than any mountain, it extends past the horizon, and it is a very important element in the earth's geography. Without the atmosphere, the many variations in weather and climate that we know on the earth would not occur, and without those variations, different natural regions would not exist (see p. 50). Also, weather and climate affect the landforms physically through the processes of erosion and weathering (see p. 35).

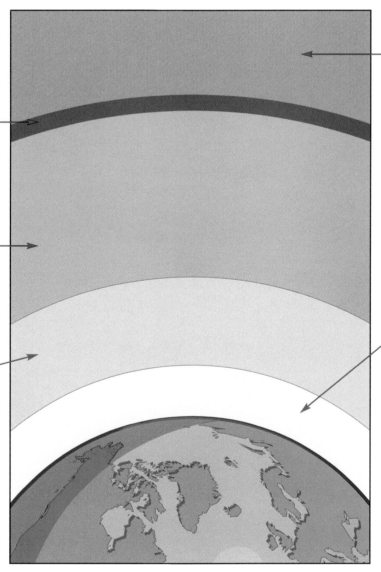

Exosphere
The border between the earth and space at about 310 miles. Satellites revolve around the earth in the exosphere.

Mesosphere
Ranges to about 50 miles. Temperatures drop to under −100°F.

Stratosphere
Stretches to about 30 miles. Icy winds blow through the lower parts, speeding supersonic jets to their destinations. Above the clouds, the air is usually dry and clear. The ozone layer, which absorbs harmful ultraviolet rays from the sun, is here.

Thermosphere
Ranges to about 400 miles above the earth's surface. Within the thermosphere, electrically-charged particles called ions make up the ionosphere. Radio waves beamed up through the atmosphere bounce back to earth from the ion layers.

Troposphere
About 12 miles thick at the equator and 5 miles thick at the poles. More than half the atmosphere's gases, water vapor, and dust particles are in the first 4 miles. We live here. Clouds and weather form here, too.

Weather and Climate

Weather is the day-to-day change in the atmosphere around us. The weather in a place varies constantly. It can be sunny and warm one day, cool and cloudy the next. Some days it rains, others it snows. Although many factors determine weather, two of the most important are temperature and precipitation (rain, snow, sleet, hail, or drizzle). The third most important factor is wind.

   Climate is the usual weather in an area over a long period of time. Some words that describe different climates are *tropical, temperate,* and *arctic.* (See also Biomes, pp. 51–56).

HEAT

Most of the heat on Earth comes from the sun. (The rest radiates outward from the very hot interior of the earth.) The heat from the sun begins as sunlight passing through the atmosphere and being absorbed into the earth. It then changes to heat and rises from the surface of the earth to warm the atmosphere. This warming of the atmosphere near the earth's surface helps create wind systems and the patterns of weather.

   The most important cause of weather is heat in the atmosphere. But not all sunlight that enters the earth's atmosphere is converted to heat. Some of the light is reflected back into space from the white tops of clouds and tiny particles of ice and water in the atmosphere. Some of the light reaches the surface of the earth and reflects off snow, water, and other reflective surfaces. Plants with green leaves absorb some of the light and change it into sugar and starch in the process called **photosynthesis**. The rest of the light is absorbed into the earth, converted into heat, and radiated back into the atmosphere, where its rising and cooling help create wind and weather.

> Dalol, Ethiopia, has the highest annual average temperature on Earth— 94°F. Nedostupnosti Polyus, Antarctica, has the coldest annual average temperature— ⁻72°F. Nedostupnosti Polyus means "inaccessible pole."

AIR PRESSURE

The weight of the atmosphere pressing down on the earth is called **air pressure**. Because warm air is less dense than cold air, warm air forms areas of low air pressure and cold air forms areas of high pressure. High pressure usually means clear skies and sunny weather. Low pressure usually means cloudy, rainy, or snowy weather.

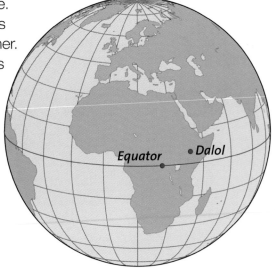

Equator • Dalol

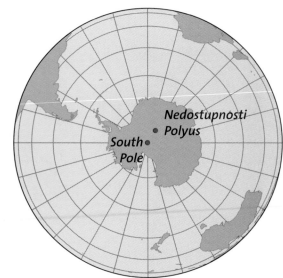

Nedostupnosti • Polyus
South •
Pole

Weather Fronts

Cold Front
Cold air moves in on an area of warm air. The heavier cold air slides underneath the lighter warm air mass and pushes it up. **Clouds** and *thunderstorms* often form.

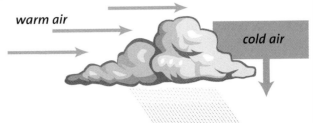

Warm Front
Warm air moves in on an area of cold air. The lighter warm air slides over the heavy, cold air, creating a front with a gentle slope. Clouds form, usually leading to some form of **precipitation**.

Stationary Front
Cold and warm air masses meet, but neither moves in on the other. Clouds often form at the boundary.

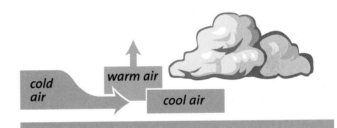

Occluded Fronts
When warm air is trapped between cold and cool air, it is forced upward. Clouds and precipitation usually result.

In places where the sun's rays reach the earth most directly and for the longest periods of time, the climate is warmer than in other places. Likewise, the coldest places are located where the sun's rays reach the earth less directly and for shorter periods of time.

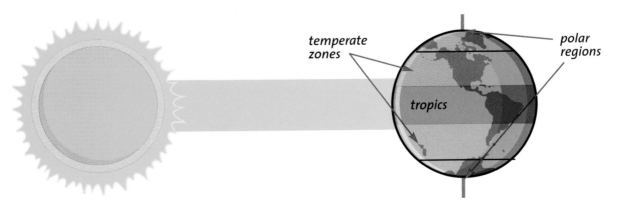

Water Heaters: Land and Ocean Temperatures

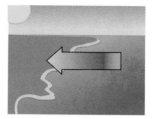

In summer, the cooler water cools the air that moves from the sea to the coast.

Oceans heat up more slowly than land masses. They also cool down more slowly. That means that in the summer the ocean is cooler than the land. It cools the air above it. This cool ocean air moves across the coastal land, keeping it cool. In winter, the water is warmer than the land, so the ocean air helps warm the air over coastal land. Temperatures vary less from summer to winter near oceans than they do in the middle of a continent.

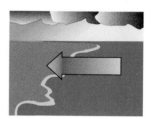

In winter, the warmer water warms the air that moves from the sea to the coast.

AIR

When air moves between areas of high and low pressure, **wind** results. The greater the difference in the pressure, the greater the speed of the wind. But air doesn't move in a straight line from one area to another. Instead, winds circle areas of high and low pressure, moving in opposite directions.

Warm air rises at the equator, and winds move in from north and south to take its place. The warm air cools and falls at around 30 degrees of latitude north and south, returning to the equator to replace other rising air. This circulation helps to cause similar air movements between 30 and 60 degrees latitude and between 60 degrees and the poles. The winds do not blow directly north and south because the earth's rotation skews them at an angle.

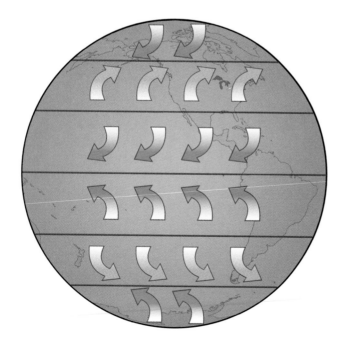
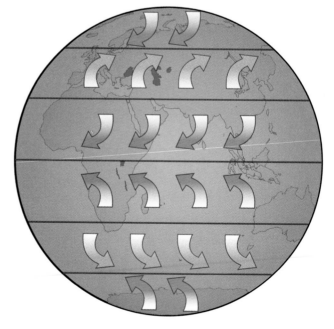

Prevailing wind patterns around the earth

HURRICANES, TORNADOES, TYPHOONS, AND CYCLONES

Hurricanes, *tornadoes*, *typhoons*, and *cyclones* are spirals of air moving around areas of intense low pressure.

Hurricanes are large storms that occur over water. These dangerous storms are known for their high winds that can topple trees and lift houses off their foundations. Hurricanes that affect the United States most often occur during the late summer and form in the Atlantic Ocean, Caribbean Sea, and Gulf of Mexico. The warm air circulating over the warm waters creates areas of low pressure. The winds surrounding the center, or eye, of the hurricane whip into speeds of 70 miles per hour and more. The eye remains calm. In countries bordering the Indian Ocean, hurricanes are called *cyclones*, although a cyclone means any large scale circular wind pattern that moves clockwise in the Southern Hemisphere and counterclockwise in the Northern Hemisphere. *Typhoon* is the name given to hurricanes that occur in the Pacific Ocean.

Tornadoes are spiral storms that occur only over land, most often forming over the Great Plains and in the upper Midwest of the United States from late spring until fall.

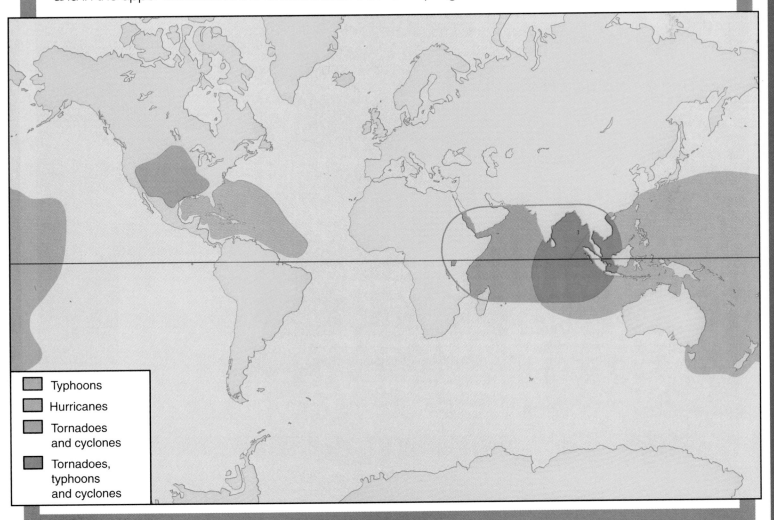

- Typhoons
- Hurricanes
- Tornadoes and cyclones
- Tornadoes, typhoons and cyclones

47

Water in the Air

Water and heat work together to create different weather conditions. Heat warms water in lakes, rivers, and oceans. The water **evaporates**, or changes from liquid to a gas called **water vapor**. Water vapor cools and condenses into droplets in the atmosphere to form clouds, fog, or ice crystals. These droplets grow heavier and fall back to the earth in the form of precipitation—rain, snow, sleet, hail, or drizzle. Warm air can hold more water vapor than cold air. That means that the humidity—or the amount of water vapor in the air—is usually greater on warm days than on cold ones.

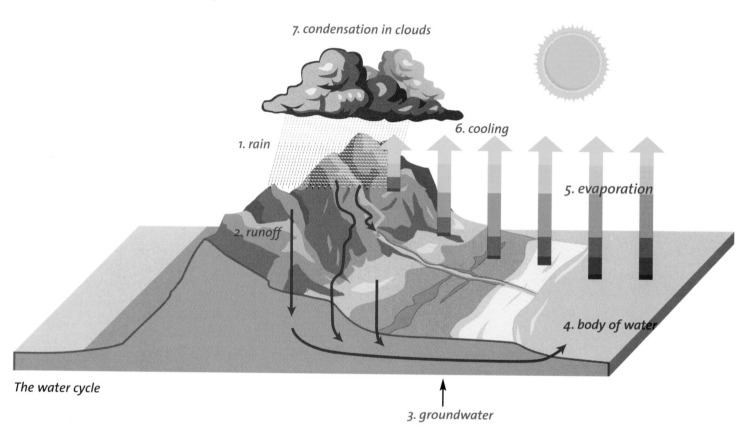

The water cycle

7. condensation in clouds
1. rain
6. cooling
5. evaporation
2. runoff
4. body of water
3. groundwater

On any day, about four trillion (4,000,000,000,000) gallons of water—about ten times the amount of water in all the world's rivers—are in the atmosphere in the form of water vapor.

The amount of moisture in the air is called *humidity*. Humidity is referred to in percentages. For example, when the air is completely filled with water vapor, the humidity is 100 percent. When the air is holding about half the water vapor it can hold, the humidity is measured at 50 percent.

Insulation: CLOUDS AND CLIMATE

Insulation prevents heat from passing into or out of an area. Your coat insulates your body, keeping your body heat in. The thick walls of a refrigerator keep the cold air inside and prevent the warm air outside from getting in.

Clouds insulate the earth. During the day they act as shields reflecting the sun's light and keep much of it from reaching the surface of the earth. At night, they act as blankets, reflecting heat leaving the earth's surface downward again. So cloudy skies tend to bring smaller swings of temperature from day to night than clear skies.

Winds at Sea

The warm and cold winds that blow across the earth don't just move air. They also push surface water along as waves. These become ocean currents, some warm and others cold. Warm and cold currents, like winds, affect the weather and climate in different places on the earth. (See also ocean currents map, p. 38.)

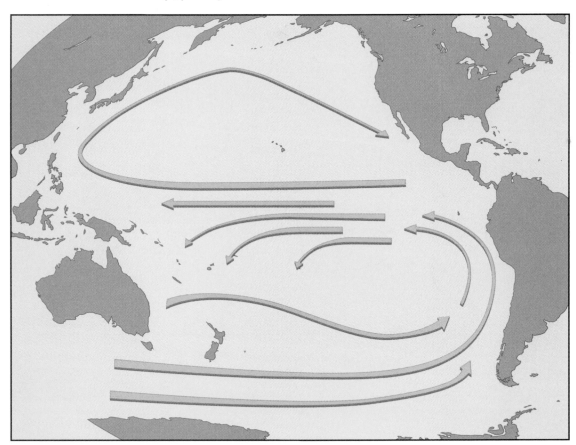

This map shows the pattern of winds over the Pacific Ocean.

The Natural Regions of the World

Land Biomes

The earth can be divided into about ten different natural regions, or **land biomes**. Each biome is unique, with a special mixture of physical features—landforms, bodies of water, and climate—and their own forms of plant and animal life.

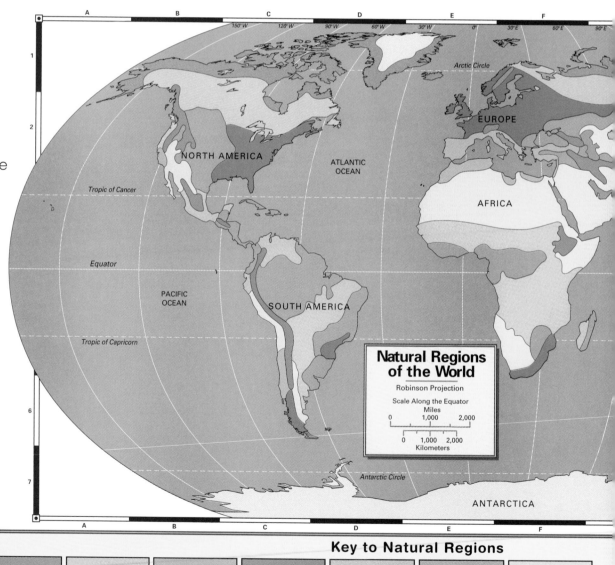

Natural Regions of the World

Robinson Projection

Scale Along the Equator
Miles
0   1,000   2,000

0   1,000   2,000
Kilometers

Key to Natural Regions

Tropical Rain Forest
Thick trees, mostly with broad leaves that stay green all year; hot and wet year-round

Tropical Grassland
Some trees among tall grasses; hot with both wet and dry seasons

Mediterranean
Wide open forests, some clumps of trees; many shrubs, herbs, and grasses; hot, dry summers, cool-to-mild winters

Temperate Forest
Mixed forests; trees that lose their leaves in winter; also trees with needles that stay green year-round; cool to cold in winter, warm in summer

Cool Forest
Mostly trees with needles that stay green year-round; some trees that lose their leaves in winter; long, cold winters, cool-to-mild summers

Cool Grassland
Prairies with tall, thick grasses and higher lands with shorter grass; cool in winter, warm in summer; drier than forest regions

Desert
Sand or completely bare soil; very few plants; in some areas, patches of grass, cactus, and bushes; very little rain

50

Chapter 2 The Biomes

Tropical Rain Forests

Tropical rain forests are warm, wet biomes near or at the equator, where more species of plants and animals flourish than in all other biomes combined.

Hundreds of varieties of trees grow in tropical rain forests, most of them hardwoods. Although the warm, wet conditions encourage luxurious growth, the trees grow so close together that they have to fight for the light they need to grow. To catch more light, trees grow very tall, and the upper branches spread out over a wide area. The tops of trees grow close together, weaving a thick layer of leaves and branches called the forest canopy. The canopy is so thick that little sunlight gets through to the rain forest floor. Between the canopy and the floor grows a layer of shrubs and small trees that rises about ten to 50 feet above the floor. This layer is called the understory. Some trees are very tall, and their branches and leaves tower at the top of the canopy. These are emergent trees, and are usually hardwoods, such as mahogany, rosewood, and ebony.

Because the floor of the rain forest is dark and damp, plants that require sunlight do not grow quickly. The few plants that grow there have broad, flat leaves to absorb as much sunlight as possible. Their leaves have waxy surfaces and pointed tips to allow water to run off easily. Other plants along the floor include vines that grow on top of understory shrubs and up tree trunks toward the light in the canopy.

Plant life is richer in the canopy than on the floor, as is the animal life. Reptiles, amphibians, birds, and mammals live together in the treetops of the rain forest. These tree-dwelling, or *arboreal*, animals include frogs, snakes, termites, eagles, toucans, parrots, flying squirrels, leopards, bats, and monkeys.

180° E

H   I   J

ASIA

PACIFIC OCEAN

AUSTRALIA

Tundra	Arctic	High Mountain
Rolling plains with no trees; patches of short grass, moss, and small flowering plants	Frozen desert, covered with ice all year; no plant life	Many different climates, depending on location; can have tropical forests at the bottom; cool forests in the middle; cold tundra higher up; snow and ice at the top

Average Daytime Temperature: 80° F
Average Nighttime Temperature: 70° F
Average Annual Rainfall: 100–200 inches

Tropical Grasslands

Tropical grasslands, often called **savannas**, are biomes located inland at or near the equator.

The seasons in tropical grasslands are called the wet season and the dry season. Because it's hot year-round, the seasons are determined by variations in rainfall, not temperature.

Few plants survive here except for tough grasses and a few hardy types of trees, among them baobabs and acacia, which have thick trunks, deep roots, and waxy, spiny leaves. These features allow them to survive the extreme drought of the dry season.

The thick grasses are food to the millions of savanna animals, among them antelopes, wildebeests, zebras, giraffes, gazelles, rhinos, buffalos, and elephants. Enormous herds of these grazers roam up and down the grasslands following the rains and searching for water and fresh grasses. Other animals, including cheetahs, leopards, and lions, follow the grazers to prey on them. Still others, including hyenas and jackals, scavenge the remains of dead or dying animals. The savannas also support hundreds of species of birds, from tiny sunbirds to eagles, and unique reptiles, amphibians, and insects.

Average Daytime Temperature: 80°F
Average Nighttime Temperature: 55°F
Average Annual Rainfall: 10–40 inches

Mediterranean Regions

Mediterranean regions, also called **chaparrals**, are coastal biomes that are cool and moist in the winter and hot and dry in the summer. These biomes support clumps of trees and some widely spread forests.

During hot summer months, drought-resistant evergreens prove the hardiest plants in this scrubland and grass biome. The leaves and stems provide moisture and nutrition for a variety of animals, most of them small enough to seek cover beneath the low branches as they nibble on leaves. Here is a home for rodents—tiny mice and rabbits—and their predators. Underground or deep in shade, lizards wait out the heat of the day. Foxes and hawks, and other predator mammals and birds, stalk and circle to make a meal of the small local fare.

The chaparral is different in winter months, when it is cooler and wetter. Then plants grow more abundantly and the animal populations surge as well. Even large grazers, such as deer, gather to nibble on the winter foliage.

Average Daytime Temperature:
90°F summer, 55°F winter
Average Nighttime Temperature:
70°F summer, 40°F winter
Average Annual Rainfall: about 10 inches

Temperate Forests

In the areas between the cold polar regions and the hot tropics of both hemispheres are **temperate forests** with warm summers and cool winters.

These temperate forests are dominated by deciduous trees, such as oak, elm, ash, maple, and birch. Evergreens are also present in these forests, including the giant sequoias of the temperate forests in northern California.

In spring and summer, the leaves of the trees provide shade for the forest floor, so temperatures remain cool. Although winters can be cold—often below freezing—the forest remains an inviting environment for many types of plants and animals, from earthworms and insects to songbirds, predator birds, deer, and foxes.

Average Daytime Temperature:
68°F summer, 32°F winter
Average Nighttime Temperature:
58°F summer, 18°F winter
Average Annual Rainfall: about 40 inches

Cool Forests

Also called **boreal** forests, **cool forests** are made up mostly of coniferous (cone-bearing) trees. The conifers grow better than other trees in these cold regions located in the extreme temperate zones and into the polar regions, where summer is short and winter is long and dark. Pine, spruce, and hemlock trees grow here, supplying cover to a few year-round residents, including birds; small mammals such as rodents, rabbits, and squirrels; and large animals such as moose, elk, caribou, and bears.

In the winter, the boreal residents tuck themselves away into natural shelters; many graze only an hour or two each day in the freezing temperatures, others hibernate during the months of deepest chill.

But spring brings summer a full complement of migratory animals, particularly birds, who seek the mild summer temperatures and abundant food in the cool forest. These animals will stay until, as summer turns to autumn, instinct tells them to move back to their tropical winter homes.

Average Daytime Temperature:
65°F summer, 20°F winter
Average Nighttime Temperature:
50°F summer, 10°F winter
Average Annual Rainfall: about 20 inches

Cool Grasslands

Cool grasslands include ***prairies*** covered in tall grasses and other regions with shorter grasses. These grasslands are drier than cool forest regions, but experience similar summer and winter temperatures.

Few of the cool grassland biomes have been left in their natural state by human beings. That's because the grasslands are excellent for farming both livestock and crops.

Instead of serving as natural grazing lands for large herds of wild animals, the grasslands are now covered in soybeans, wheat, barley, oats, and other grain crops. Populations of cows, sheep, horses, goats, and other domesticated animals feed on the coarse grasses.

Average Daytime Temperature: 75°F summer, 20°F winter
Average Nighttime Temperature: 60°F summer, 0°F winter
Average Annual Rainfall: under 25 inches

Deserts

Deserts are regions—hot or cold—where the land is covered in sand or bare soil and precipitation totals are very small, less than ten inches each year.

In most hot deserts, temperatures vary greatly, from extremely hot days to cool, even freezing, nights.

Plant and animal life in deserts is well adapted to the harsh environment. Cacti and euphorbia are typical desert plants. Called ***succulents***, these plants store water in their waxy leaves and stems. To avoid the hot days, many animals in the desert are ***nocturnal***, or active only at night. These animals burrow deep into the earth to spend the daylight hours away from the burning sun. They search for food during the cool nighttime hours. Certain types of lizards and snakes thrive in the hot desert sun, as do animals that need only a little water.

Although we often think of deserts as hot places, not all deserts are hot. The far north of Siberia in Russia and much of Antarctica are cold deserts.

Average Daytime Temperature: 100°F summer, 65°F winter*
Average Nighttime Temperature: 75°F summer, 45°F winter*
Average Annual Rainfall: under 10 inches

*Averages represent hot deserts located in tropical and temperate regions, not frozen deserts.

Tundra

Tundra biomes are extreme climates, too cold for trees to grow. While the top of the ground thaws during the warm season, a layer beneath it, about ten inches of frozen ground, never melts. It is called **permafrost**.

In this harsh biome, winter is particularly cruel. Yet a few animals remain after the others have migrated south for the winter. Lemmings, ermines, arctic foxes, wolves, musk oxen, reindeer, and polar bears grow heavy winter coats or huddle into dens to keep warm through the long, dark winter.

During the few short months of warm weather, low-growing tundra flowers bloom. Birds and insects newly arrived from the south feast on these, as do herds of moose and caribou that have traveled to the tundra from their winter homes farther south.

Average Daytime Temperature: 55°F summer, 30°F winter
Average Nighttime Temperature: 40°F summer, −10°F winter
Average Annual Rainfall: 30–45 inches

Polar Regions

The **polar regions** are frozen deserts covered in ice all year long. Because it is over land instead of water, the Antarctic is much colder than the Arctic.

The Arctic polar region (around the north pole) is a solid mass of frozen ocean water. The Antarctic polar region (around the south pole) is a mass of frozen land covered in ice and snow. Together, the areas surrounding the north and south poles are known as the **polar ice caps**.

Powerful icy winds blow across the polar ice caps, causing blizzards of snow and ice blown up from the surface. However, little snow actually falls from the skies over the ice caps because the air temperatures are too cold for moisture to evaporate and form clouds.

Only migrating animals, such as polar bears and arctic seals, are found on the Arctic ice mass. Very few animals are hearty enough to survive conditions in Antarctica. The few that do manage it live along the coasts of the continent, relying upon the sea for food and shelter. Among these remarkable animals are such birds as petrels, gulls, terns, albatrosses, and penguins. Penguins are insulated with a heavy coat of feathers over skin protected by a thick layer of fat.

In the icy north arctic seas live Arctic mammals. Here dolphins, porpoises, whales, and seals, protected by thick layers of oily fat called **blubber**, swim in the near-freezing waters.

Average Daytime Temperature:	Arctic: 30°F summer, −10°F winter
	Antarctic: 7°F summer, −80°F winter
Average Nighttime Temperature:	Arctic: 10°F summer, −20°F winter
	Antarctic: −50°F summer, −95°F winter
Average Annual Rainfall:	5–20 inches

Mountain Biomes

Because of the changes in altitude (height above sea level), high mountain environments support a variety of different climates. Depending on the location of the mountain ranges, biomes on high mountains can range from tropical rain forest to tundra and frozen desert. Mountains also help create different biomes. As warm, moist air flows from coastal regions up against mountain ranges on their **windward** sides, the air pushes upward and cools. The cooled water vapor condenses into droplets in the form of clouds. Often these droplets become large enough to fall as rain. Because moisture-carrying air is blocked by the mountain ranges, drier climates, such as plains or deserts, often form on the **leeward** sides.

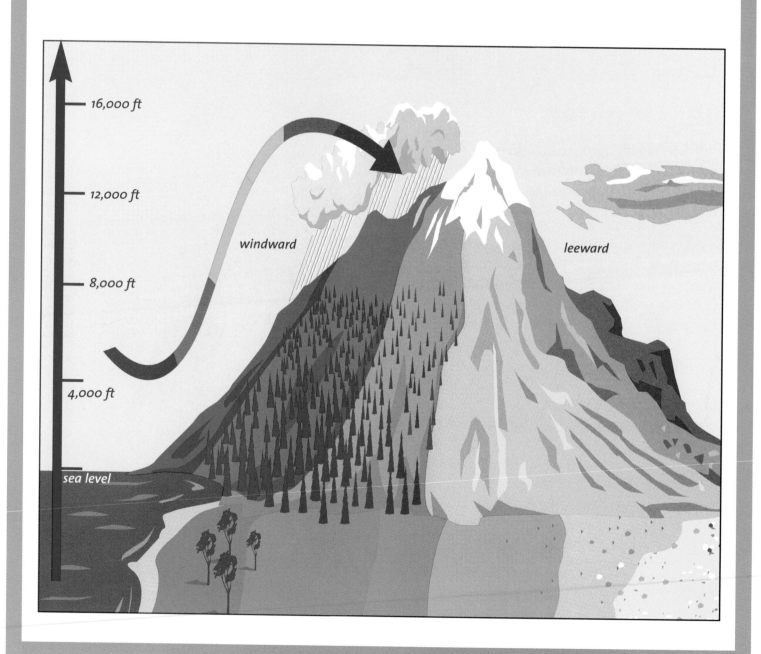

People on Land and Water

Location and Place

What Are Location and Place?

Location is where something—for example, a house, a school, a store, an airport, a mine, or a crop field—is created or built. Location is described in absolute terms (latitude and longitude) or relative terms (north of the road or near the playground). A location becomes a *place* when it is described in terms of its human or physical characteristics.

Climate and landscape, as well as religion, schools, politics, opportunities to make a living, and environmental surroundings give character to a place.

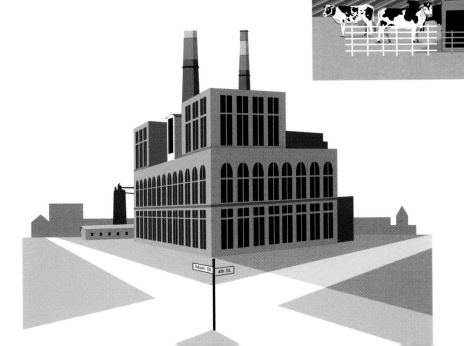

A farm and a factory are two kinds of places. Farms are usually located in the countryside. The factory on the left is located at the intersection of 4th and Main streets.

Counting People: Population

Population

Population is the total number of people who live in a particular place. Geographers study population to understand where people live and why they live there.

WORLD POPULATION GROWTH

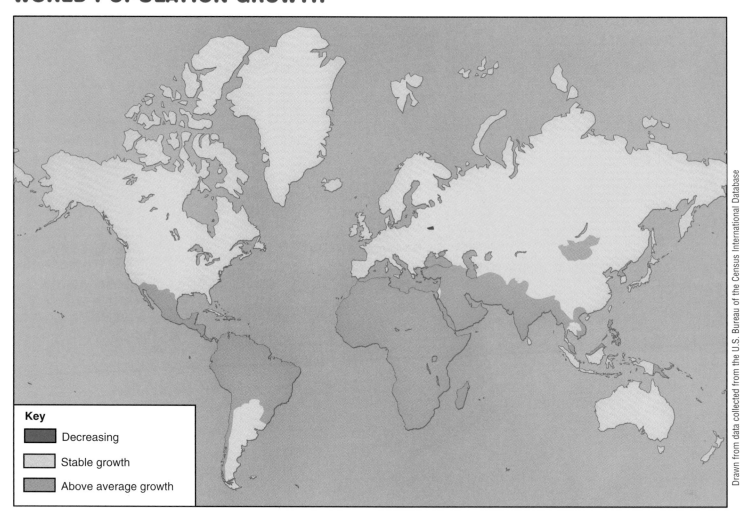

Key
- Decreasing
- Stable growth
- Above average growth

Drawn from data collected from the U.S. Bureau of the Census International Database

A map of world population growth shows areas where the number of people is growing, decreasing, or remaining about the same.

> The study of population is called *demographics*.
> Scientists who study demographics are called *demographers*.

WORLD POPULATION GROWTH, 1600–PRESENT

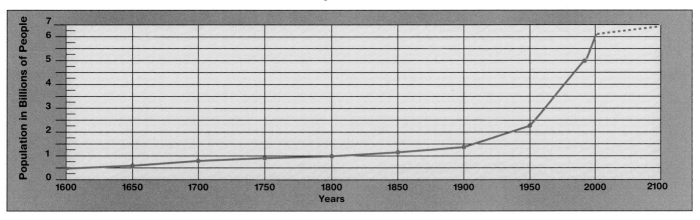

This graph shows world population in billions of people over the last 400 years.

Population Data

In studying human populations, geographers use a lot of different information called **population data**. These data include basic facts about human populations—past, present, and projected into the future.

SOME TYPES OF POPULATION DATA

1 Average family size — The average number of children in a family in a particular culture group or region

2 Birth rate — The number of babies born per year per thousand people

3 Death rate — The number of people who die per year per thousand people

4 Doubling time — The time needed for a population to increase 100 percent (double)

5 Life expectancy — The average number of years people live

6 Population growth rate — How quickly a population grows each year, measured by percentage

7 Population structure — The makeup of a population by age and gender (male or female)

> The world's population increases by about three people every second. That's nearly 200 people a minute, 10,000 people an hour, and 240,000 people a day!

POPULATION PICTURES: PROFILES AND PYRAMIDS

Geographers use graphs to compare populations in different areas. Two of the most common graphs are the **population profile** and the **population pyramid**.

POPULATION PROFILE

A **population profile** is a bar graph that shows the different age groups of a population that share something in common, such as language, dog ownership, or a school.

POPULATION PYRAMID

A **population pyramid** is a bar graph that depicts a total population by breaking it down into age groupings and gender.

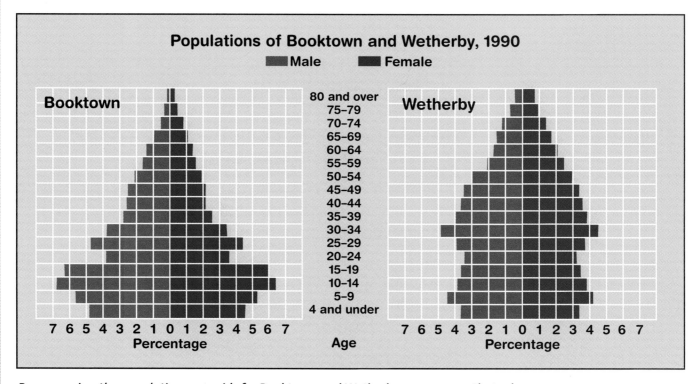

By comparing the population pyramids for Booktown and Wetherby, you can see that a larger percentage of Booktown is aged 10–19 than Wetherby. That is because the Boys' Academy of Reading, an all-male middle and high school, brings hundreds of school-age boys into Booktown each year, skewing the population in that age group.

Population Density and Distribution

Population density means how close together people live in a particular place. To find population density, divide the number of people in a place by the total area of that place.

 Population distribution or **patterns** tell geographers where most people live within a place or region.

Maps show both population density and distribution. This map shows the population density and distribution in the state of Wisconsin. More than half of the 5,000,000 residents live in cities located in the southeastern and south central parts of the state. Located in these areas are the largest cities in the state: Milwaukee, Madison, and Green Bay.

WISCONSIN POPULATION DENSITY AND DISTRIBUTION

• **Green Bay**
(app. population 102,000)

⭐ *Madison*
(app. population 208,000)

• *Milwaukee*
(app. population 597,000)

Drawn from data gathered by the U.S. Bureau of the Census

Persons per square mile

More than 100

50 to 100

25 to 50

less than 25

Urban vs. Rural

About half the earth's people live in cities and towns, called **urban areas**.
The other half live on farms or in countryside villages, called **rural areas**.

POPULATION PATTERNS: URBAN VS. RURAL

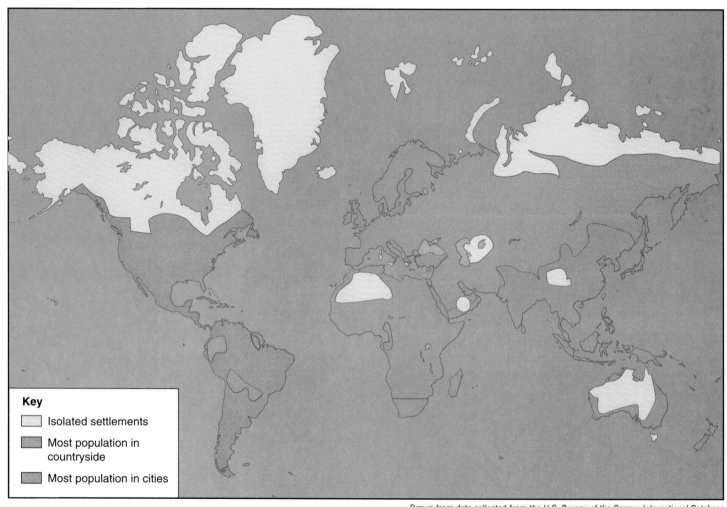

Key

Isolated settlements

Most population in countryside

Most population in cities

Drawn from data collected from the U.S. Bureau of the Census International Database

A map of population patterns shows where people live mostly in cities (urban) and where people live mostly in the countryside (rural).

A MODEL CITY, A MODEL COUNTRYSIDE

A **city**, or **metropolis**, is a large or important town. Sometimes a city grows so large that it grows into a neighboring city, forming a **megalopolis**. But no matter how big it is, a city is made up of a variety of areas.

Businesses and industries are located in the **commercial areas** of a city. Stores and service businesses often are located in **downtown** commercial areas, or the main business area of a city, called the **central business district (CBD)**. Manufacturing and heavy industry (see p. 75) are usually located along the outer edges of a city on major transportation routes (roads, waterways, trains, airports, etc.).

People's homes are located in the **residential** areas of a city. Homes are also found in the **suburbs**, or the residential districts lying just outside a city or town. Like the people who live in the residential areas of a city, people who live in the suburbs usually work in the city and benefit from the services the city offers. Beyond the suburbs are **exurbs**, sparsely populated residential areas.

Most cities are divided into **neighborhoods**, each with its own special cultural makeup. Some neighborhoods are made up of people with the same ethnic or religious background. For example, many U.S. cities have Chinese, Italian, Korean, or African-American neighborhoods. Other neighborhoods are unique because of their architecture or the era in which they were built. Many U.S. cities have preserved their "historic districts" or the "old cities" where the oldest buildings in the city stand. Still other neighborhoods are defined by physical features. Terms such as "riverside," "highlands," and "flats" are often used to describe neighborhoods within cities.

Outside cities are small towns, villages, and other rural communities, as well as farmland, forests, parks, and other tracts of land. Highways, smaller roads, waterways, railroads, and other transportation routes connect rural areas to each other and to nearby cities, states, or even foreign countries.

Towns are usually smaller than cities, but both are thickly populated areas with fixed boundaries and local governments.

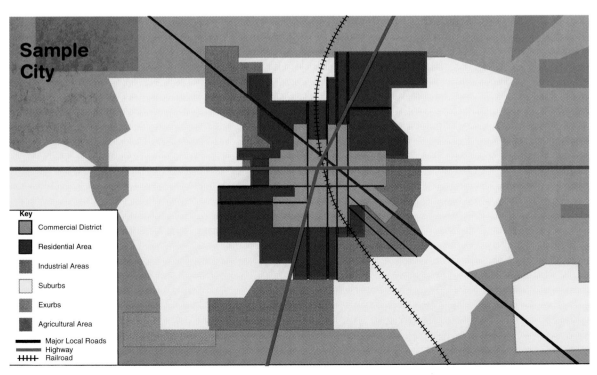

Key
- Commercial District
- Residential Area
- Industrial Areas
- Suburbs
- Exurbs
- Agricultural Area
- Major Local Roads
- Highway
- Railroad

Sample City

Like most cities, Sample City is made up of several distinct areas, including a downtown, industrial district, residential neighborhoods, and suburbs.

63

World Birth Rates: 1910–2000

Rate of Births
(per 1,000 people per year)

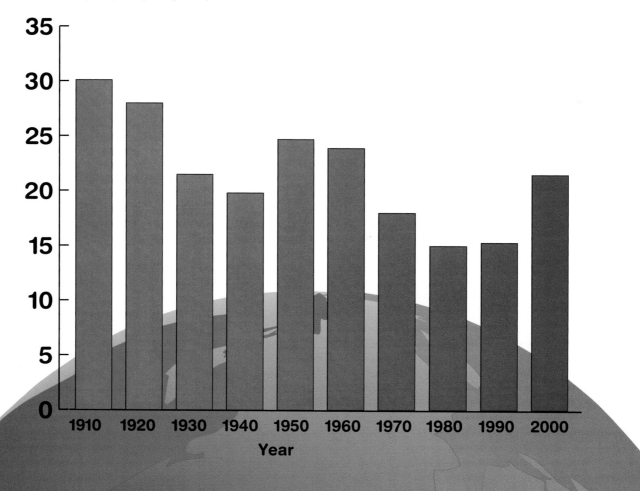

Chapter 3 Culture

What Is Culture?

Culture is a word used to describe how groups of people act: how we live, what we eat, what we believe, and how we change our environment to create communities.

Geographers who study culture try to explain how people behaved in the past compared with how we behave today. They compare the way people in different areas live their lives. They study languages, beliefs and traditions, political systems, and the technologies that bind communities together or make them different from other communities.

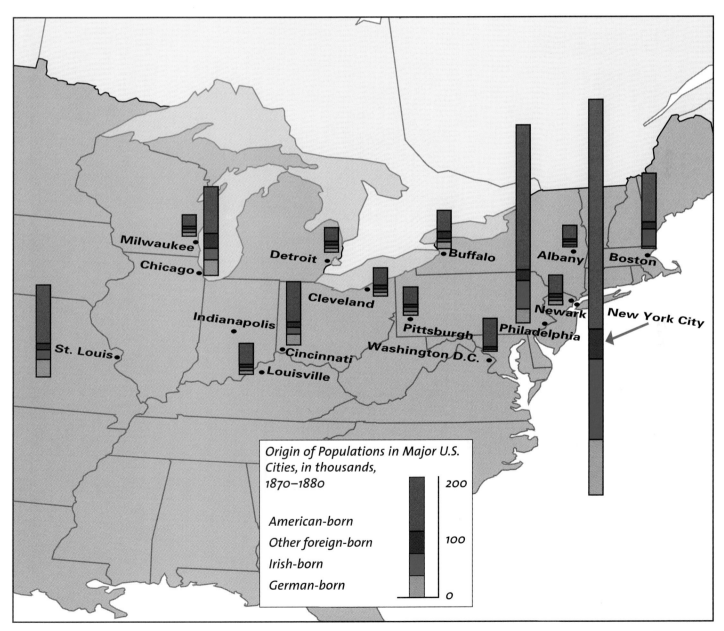

Origin of Populations in Major U.S. Cities, in thousands, 1870–1880

- American-born
- Other foreign-born
- Irish-born
- German-born

This cultural map compares the Irish and German populations to other foreign-born and American-born citizens of major northeastern and midwestern American cities in the 1870s.

THE CULTURAL MOSAIC

Geographers consider each culture group to consist of different pieces, like the pieces in a **mosaic**, a picture made by fitting together separate tiles, stones, or glass pieces. Viewed together, the pieces that make up a culture create a picture of that culture, called a **cultural mosaic**.

Elements of the cultural mosaic can be witnessed in a typical American suburban backyard. The types of clothes we wear, the food we eat, the games we play, and the architecture of our homes are all pieces of our cultural mosaic.

Culture Basics

1. **Language (see below)**
2. **Beliefs and traditions (see pp. 68–70)**
3. **Arts and crafts (see p. 71)**
4. **Political systems (see p. 74)**
5. **Technologies (see p. 75)**

Language

Language is the use of voice sounds, gestures, and written symbols to communicate thoughts and feelings.

> The five languages most widely spoken in the world today are Mandarin Chinese, English, Hindi, Spanish, and Russian.

LANGUAGE FAMILIES

More than 2,800 languages are spoken in the world today. These languages have been grouped into several *language families*. Here are some of the main groups.

FAMILY/GROUP	PRINCIPAL LANGUAGES
Afro-Asian	Amharic, Arabic, Berber, Hebrew
Black African	Includes Khoisan, Niger-Kordofanian, and Nilo-Saharan language families
Dravidian	Tamil, Telugu
Indo-European	Albanian, Armenian, Belorussian, Bengali, Bulgarian, Croatian, Czech, Danish, Dutch, English, French, German, Greek, Gujarati, Hindi, Icelandic, Iranian, Italian, Latvian, Lithuanian, Macedonian, Marathi, Norwegian, Polish, Portuguese, Punjabi, Romanian, Russian, Serbian, Slovak, Slovenian, Spanish, Swedish, Ukrainian, Urdu
Korean and Japanese	Korean and Japanese
Malayo-Poynesian	Indonesian, Malagasy, Malay, Maori, Pilipino, Tagalog
Mon-Khmer	Khmer and Laotian
Sino-Tibetan	Burmese, Chinese, Lao, Tibetan, Thai, Vietnamese
Uralic-Altaic	Estonian, Finnish, Hungarian, Turkish

Slang is a variation of language used instead of standard vocabulary. It is usually used to provide emphasis or humor in speech and, sometimes, in writing. A *dialect* is a variation of a standard language spoken by a particular group of people. A dialect differs from standard language in grammar, vocabulary, or pronunciation, or in any combination of the three.

LANGUAGE BARRIERS

Throughout early history, mountains have stopped the spread of language. So have large bodies of water, deserts, and thick jungles. Because people couldn't cross these barriers easily, groups of people on opposite sides developed languages separately. So, people on one side of a geographic barrier might speak a language different from people on the other. Today these boundaries are no longer difficult to cross, yet they help explain the diversity of world languages.

More than 1,000 Native American languages are spoken in isolated areas throughout the Americas.

WORLD LANGUAGE FAMILIES

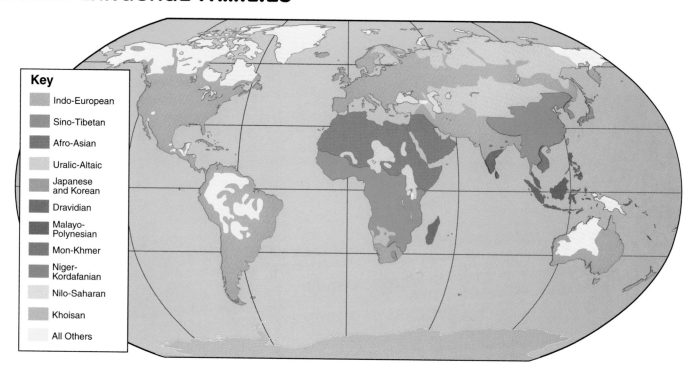

Key
- Indo-European
- Sino-Tibetan
- Afro-Asian
- Uralic-Altaic
- Japanese and Korean
- Dravidian
- Malayo-Polynesian
- Mon-Khmer
- Niger-Kordafanian
- Nilo-Saharan
- Khoisan
- All Others

Beliefs and Traditions: Religions, Customs, and Arts and Crafts

Beliefs are the attitudes, ideas, and world views held by a person or a group of people. Every culture has a set of beliefs, or a **belief system**. This system is made up of three basic elements:

1 Religion — A belief in and legends about a god or gods who created the world and affect peoples' lives

2 Customs and manners — The traditions people have or ways people act or behave in a group

3 Arts and crafts — The clothing, music, arts, architecture, tools, etc., used by a group

RELIGION

Over the centuries, people have believed in many religions. Today, dozens of religions are practiced in the world. However, five major religions are the most widely practiced.

MAJOR WORLD RELIGIONS (In order of approximate date of origin)

1 Hinduism
Begun about 1500 B.C. in India. Hindus believe in many gods and in reincarnation (rebirth of the soul after death). Today, Hinduism is practiced by 900 million people primarily in India, Nepal, Malaysia, Indonesia, Guyana, Suriname, and Sri Lanka.

2 Judaism
Begun about 1300 B.C. among the Hebrew people in the Middle East. Judaism was the first religion founded on a belief in one god rather than a group of gods. Today, Judaism is practiced by 14 million people throughout the world, primarily in Israel, Europe, and the United States.

3 Buddhism
Begun about 525 B.C. by Siddhartha Gautama (Buddha), c. 563–480, in India. Buddhists follow the Hindu belief in reincarnation, and they work to gain inner peace, called nirvana. Today, Buddhism is practiced by approximately 360 million people throughout Asia, from Sri Lanka to Japan.

4 Christianity
Begun in the first century in the Middle East among Jews who believed that Jesus of Nazareth was the divine son of god. Today, Christianity is practiced by approximately 2 billion people throughout the world, primarily in Europe, North America, South America, and Africa, as well as in pockets of Asia.

5 Islam
Begun in A.D. 622 in the Middle East by followers of Muhammad. Islam includes many of the features of Judaism and Christianity, including the belief in one god, which Moslems call Allah. Today, Islam is practiced by 1.3 billion people, primarily in the western and northern countries of Africa, throughout the Middle East, Central Asia, western China, Malaysia, Indonesia, the Philippines, and the United States.

The rest of the world's population, approximately 1.8 billion people, practice other religions or no religion.

CUSTOMS AND MANNERS

Customs are the usual habits of a group of people. **Manners**, or norms, are the habits considered to be polite among a group of people. Both customs and manners are the result of what a group considers important: its values. For example, when a young person offers a seat to an older person, the custom demonstrates the value of respect for one's elders.

GREETINGS!
Manners, Meanings, and Cultural Differences

What is accepted as polite behavior in one place isn't necessarily so in another.

Waving with the palm of the hand facing out is a gesture of greeting in America and most European cultures. In Turkey and Greece, however, the gesture is called "The Hand of Moutza," and is considered a serious insult.

In the United States, people often shake hands as a greeting or when they are introduced to new people. In Japan and India, touch is not used in greetings. In Japan, people bow to acknowledge new contacts or to express respect to old friends. In India, people touch their palms together, prayer-style, to show welcome.

Sticking out the tongue is considered rude in the United States, but among the Aborigines in Australia, it is a sign of greeting and affection. In China, it is a sign of embarrassment.

ARTS AND CRAFTS

Art communicates the values and beliefs of a culture in what that culture finds beautiful. It can include paintings, sculpture, plays, poems, dance, photographs, movies, novels, and music.

   Crafts refers to useful items and the methods used to make them. Crafts include sewing, weaving, tools for cooking, farming, mining, manufacturing, and the design and construction of buildings (architecture).

> **All the art forms—visual arts, music, literature, and dance—together are called the fine arts.**

Culture Crafts

Hand-woven baskets, woolen blankets and rugs, pottery, and ivory needles—among many other items—have been used for centuries in different cultures throughout the world. Created for everyday use, many of these items are now considered art objects. That means their value is measured both in their usefulness and their beauty.

HOME SWEET HOME
The Architecture of Houses

People in different cultural groups tend to build different kinds of houses. The differences include:

1. Building materials: some cultures build homes of wood, others of stone, and others of earth. People build homes with the materials available in their geographical regions.

2. Beauty: people build homes that look pleasing to them, homes that fit their idea of beauty. In Europe, new homes are often built to look like those that have stood in villages for hundreds of years. Among the Bedouin of North Africa, homes are not permanent structures, but brilliantly colored tents festooned with tassels and fringes.

3. Use: people build homes primarily for shelter but also to fit the way they live. A Masai cattle herder needs a place within his home, or **shamba**, to corral livestock. An Inuit needs shelter from the Arctic winds as well as access to fishing. An American suburbanite needs to be near transportation to the city. Homes are also designed to suit different climates and amounts of space. For example, many houses in cold climates are insulated between the inside and outside walls, floors, and ceilings. In tropical climates, walls made of a single layer of bamboo or reeds provide shelter from the hot sun.

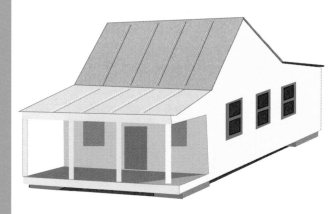

Plantation-style houses have been built around the world by European settlers. This particular style of house, however, is most often seen in agricultural or tropical regions.

Teepees were once home to some of the members of the Plains nations of Native Americans.

Houses built along the rivers and rice paddies of Asia are often built on stilts to protect dwellers from rising and falling water levels.

Food! Glorious Food!

What people in a group eat is part of their culture. The food culture is created by tastes and influenced by religion and customs. A group's diet is also determined by what it can grow or raise. Climate, too, influences how people build their kitchens and prepare their foods.

Location determines dietary factors in many cultures. However, nowadays, because of excellent transportation and storage, canned goods are found in the homes of Arctic Inuits and frozen meals in the homes of people in desert regions.

Cuisine means a particular style of cooking or preparing food. Cuisine is determined by everything from taste to climate, farming, and location. For example, the cuisines of Asia use rice as a main ingredient. In Italian cuisine, wheat flour noodles called pasta are common. Cuisine is another way of saying "food culture." Today, with mass communication, migration, and transportation, many cuisines are available all over the world. Chinese and Italian cuisines, for example, are enjoyed by people in restaurants all over North America. Once an American phenomenon, fast foods, such as hamburgers and fries, are available in cities as far away as Beijing, China, and São Paulo, Brazil.

Political Systems

Political systems are **governments**, or the ruling bodies of the world's peoples. People who live under one government form a **country** or **nation**.

What Is Government?

A political system or *government* provides a set of laws and rules. There are many types of political systems, including:

Anarchy	**No government or organized authority.**
Confederacy	**An alliance of separately governed states.**
Democracy	**A nation in which power rests with the people and is exercised directly by them or their elected representatives.**
Dictatorship	**A nation in which absolute power is controlled by a person whose position is not inherited.**
Empire	**A group of nations or territories ruled by one leader or country.**
Monarchy	**A nation ruled by a supreme sovereign, such as a king, queen, or emperor. In most monarchies, the rulers inherit their power. A constitutional monarchy is a system in which a king or queen is the head of state in a country ruled by a separate government.**
Parliamentary Government	**An assembly of persons, not necessarily elected, who write the laws of a nation or state.**
Republic	**A nation without a monarch and, in modern times, usually led by a president.**

How People Live

Chapter 4

The Hunter-Gatherers

In ancient societies, people lived as **hunter-gatherers**. In some places today, they still do. That means they hunt, fish, and forage from the wild to find food.

Subsistence Farmers

To feed themselves, humans learned to sow plants and grow crops as well as to hunt and gather food. Over time, farmers learned to raise enough food to feed themselves.

Farmers who raise just enough food to feed themselves and their families are called **subsistence farmers**. Subsistence farming is still common in several parts of the world. In other parts, farming has become an industry or commercial activity (see below).

INDUSTRY & TECHNOLOGY

Industry means making products not simply for your use or your family's, but for sale to other people. Industries are divided into two categories: light and heavy.

Light industries use lightweight raw materials to make clothes, food products, plants and flowers, furniture, and other consumer goods

Heavy industries produce machines that do big jobs, such as cranes, oil derricks, cars, ships, airplanes, and farm equipment

There are many different types of light and heavy industries, but most fall into one of five categories:

1. **Agriculture**
2. **Mining**
3. **Forestry**
4. **Fishing and fishery**
5. **Manufacturing**

Technology is the use of scientific knowledge, usually to improve industry and commerce. Technology includes the machines and other tools used to work in a variety of industries, manufacturing (see p. 81), and arts and crafts (see p. 71).

Agriculture

Agriculture means farming. Farming began more than 10,000 years ago. Unlike hunter-gatherers who roamed from one place to another to find food, farmers built permanent homes and farmed the same land in the same area year after year.

Most of the food we eat and many of the materials for the things we use are grown on farms.

Some farms only grow plants, or crops, for food (fresh vegetables and fruits) or manufacture (wheat for flour, soybeans for meat substitutes, cotton for fabrics, corn for feed, etc.). Other farms use the land to graze animals. These are called livestock farms, and include farms where animals are raised to be processed into meat or to provide milk for dairy products (milk, cream, butter, cheese) and eggs. Some farms produce both crops and livestock. (These are called mixed farms.)

Old MacDonald Had a Farm

Old MacDonald had a farm—but just what kind of farm was it?

cooperative farm	Farm owned and operated by a group of farmers for the benefit of each individual involved.
corporate farm	Farm owned by a corporation, usually producing goods for sale in stores under a company label.
crop farm	Farm that raises food crops for harvest, such as vegetables, fruits, or grains.
dairy farm	Farm specializing in the production of milk, cheese, butter, and other dairy products.
family farm	Farm owned and operated by a family as a private business.
livestock farm	Farm specializing in raising animals, such as chickens, pigs, cows, goats, or buffalo, for egg, dairy, or meat production.
mixed farm	Farm where both livestock and crops are raised.
ranch	Farm specializing in one type of crop or livestock, such as a cattle ranch, mink ranch, or deer ranch.
subsistence farm	Farm on which food and other products necessary for life are grown by one family for its own use.
commercial farm	Farm specializing in products for sale to a wide market and intended to make profits from sales instead of products for family use.
plantation	Large farm or estate in a tropical or semitropical area, often specializing in commercial crops, such as cotton, tobacco, rice, sugar cane, coffee, or tea.
truck farm	Farm close to a city that specializes in vegetables, fruit, and other cash crops.
herding farm	Farm that uses large areas of land, usually arid, for herding goats, camels, sheep, and/or cattle.

World Agriculture

Estimated World Agricultural Workforce in 2000

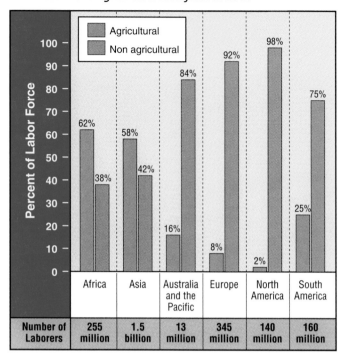

| Number of Laborers | 255 million | 1.5 billion | 13 million | 345 million | 140 million | 160 million |

Estimated World Livestock Production by Region in 2000

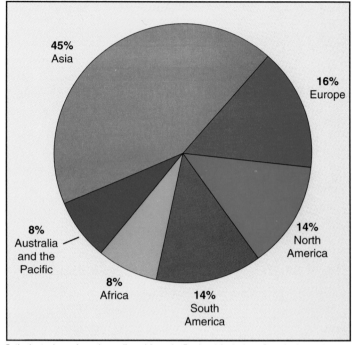

Both charts drawn from data collected from the Food and Agriculture Organization of the United Nations (2003) and *CIA World Factbook* (2003).

More than half the labor force—or almost two billion people—in Asia and Africa work in agriculture, whereas only approximately 3 percent—or about 88 million people—work in agriculture in the rest of the world. Yet these 88 million people produce almost half the world's crops. By comparing these graphs, you might conclude that most of the farming in Asia and Africa is subsistence farming, not commercial farming.

Mining

Mining means taking rocks and minerals out of the earth. Many different rocks and minerals are mined, although they all fall into one of four categories:

Category	Example
metals	iron, lead, gold, silver, platinum
gemstones	diamonds, emeralds, rubies, sapphires, amethyst, lapis lazuli, jade
fossil fuels	natural gas, oil, coal
conglomerates	rock, sand, gravel

Some rocks and minerals are harder than others. The hardness is measured on the Mohs scale, a scale devised by the German scientist Friedrich Mohs. It ranks all rocks from 1 to 10.

MOHS SCALE

Softest	1	Talc
	2	Gypsum
	3	Calcite
	4	Fluorite
	5	Apatite
	6	Feldspar
	7	Quartz
	8	Topaz
	9	Corundum
Hardest	10	Diamond

Which Mine Is Mine? Different Types of Mining

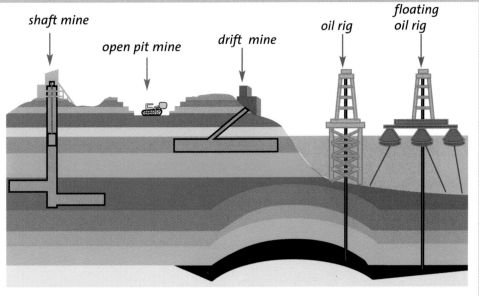

shaft mine

open pit mine

drift mine

oil rig

floating oil rig

Mining occurs above ground, deep underground, and even under the seas and oceans.

Some mineral resources are running low. If we continue to use minerals at our current rate, silver, gold, copper, natural gas, oil, iron ore, and uranium could be in short supply by 2050. However, because we recognize the danger, some people are using minerals more carefully. Also, geologists are searching for new deposits of these precious minerals on land and in the oceans.

Forestry

Forestry is the growing, maintaining, and harvesting of forests. Forests provide us with wood, which is used for building materials, furniture, paper, fuel, gums and resins, waxes, and medicines.

The world's forests come in many sizes and are filled with many different types of trees.

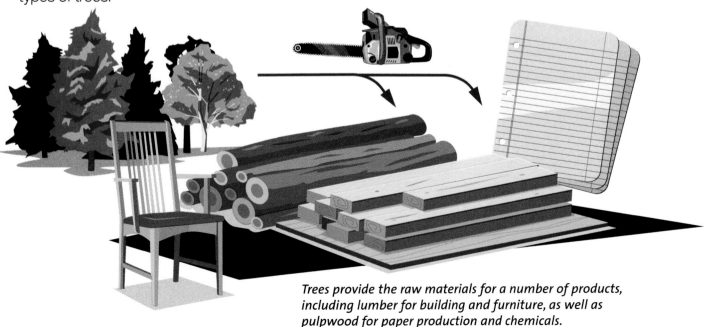

Trees provide the raw materials for a number of products, including lumber for building and furniture, as well as pulpwood for paper production and chemicals.

79

Fishing and Fisheries

The business of fishing is called **fishery**, and includes not only the catching and farming of fish and other aquatic animals, but also their processing and selling. Fishing is big business around the world. Nearly 80 million tons of sea animals are caught each year.

Manufacturing

Manufacturing means making new products from both raw materials and recycled materials. **Raw materials** are the natural products used to make new products. **Recycled materials** are the glass, metal, plastic, and paper collected from trash that are processed and reused to make new products.

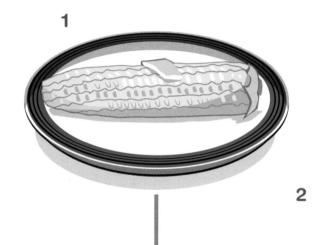

1

2

3

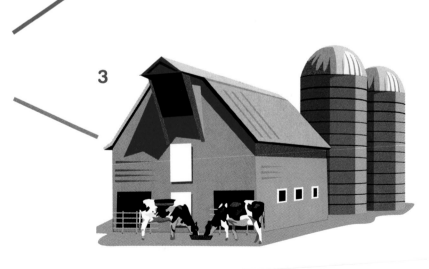

Corn is a versatile raw material. It is used as: 1. a food crop; 2. a raw material for producing corn oil and other processed foods and materials; and 3. a feed crop to support livestock.

A Brief History of Manufacturing

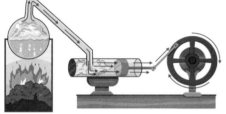

Machines such as the spinning wheel made cottage industries possible.

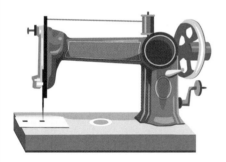

James Watt patented his steam engine in 1769, and the Industrial Revolution began.

The sewing machine made the creation of clothes easier for homemakers. It also made the garment industry possible because clothes could be mass-produced with the aid of this time-saving machine.

Before the 1700s, most people manufactured goods for their own use in their homes. People wove fleece and plant fibers into fabrics and made their own clothes. They caught fish and raised crops, and preserved and canned them. They cut trees to burn as fuel and to use as lumber to build houses, barns, fences, and more.

Later, people made things for other people from within their homes. For example, a tailor would sew not only for himself or herself, but also for those who paid for the service. A farmer might grow extra crops to sell at a farm stand, or a lumberer might fell logs for other people to build with or burn as firewood. People still manufacture products in their homes or in small local factories. These home-based manufacturing operations are called **cottage industries**.

In Europe, the early 1700s brought machines that made work easier and the production of manufactured products quicker and cheaper. The most important of these machines was improved and patented by the British inventor James Watt in 1769. It was the steam engine, and it brought about a change in the way people in Europe and the New World made products. This period of change is called the **Industrial Revolution**.

With the Industrial Revolution came many changes in the world of manufacturing and business. For example, instead of making one product at a time, the machines of the Industrial Revolution allowed for **mass production**, or the creation of many of the same products at the same time.

Many factory owners earned a great deal of money by selling mass-produced products. They built huge factories to make more and more products. To operate these factories, they hired many people. In fact, huge numbers of people moved into cities and factory towns during the Industrial Revolution to find work, live, and raise families.

Then, as today, businesses built or bought up other factories in different towns, cities, or even different states or countries. Companies with factories in two or more countries are called **multinational companies**.

Many items are produced on assembly lines, where different workers are responsible for separate tasks in the creation of a product. Cars are mass-produced, usually on assembly lines.

150°W 120°W 90°W 60°W 30°W

Beaufort Sea

**GREENLAND
(KALAALLIT NUNAAT)
(DENMARK)**

AI
*Greenland
Sea*

*Baffin
Bay*

Arctic Circle

ICELAND DENM.

THE NETHERLAND

BELGIU

**ALASKA
(U.S.)**

*Hudson
Bay*

CANADA

ATLANTIC
OCEAN

**UNITED
KINGDOM**

IRELAND

FR.

*Gulf of
Alaska*

○LUXEMBOURG
SWITZERLAND
○LIECHTENSTEIN
SLOVENIA
CROATIA
○MONACO
○ANDORRA

M.

BOSNIA AND HERZEGOVINA
PORTUGAL
SPAIN

○VATIC
SERB
MONTE

UNITED STATES OF AMERICA

30°N

MEXICO

*Gulf of
Mexico*

DOMINICAN
REPUBLIC
PUERTO RICO (U.S.)
VIRGIN ISLANDS (U.S., U.K.)

ALB
MACEI

ALG

*CANARY
ISLANDS*
(SPAIN)

MOROCCO

○Bahamas

CUBA

Tropic of Cancer

**HAWAIIAN
ISLANDS**
(U.S.)

PACIFIC
OCEAN

HAITI

JAMAICA

*WESTERN
SAHARA*
(disputed)

MAURITANIA

MALI

●St. Kitts and Nevis
●Antigua and Barbuda
●Dominica
●St. Lucia
●St. Vincent
AND THE GRENADINES
●Barbados
●Grenada
●Trinidad and Tobago

●Cape Verde

BELIZE
GUATEMALA
El Salvador
Honduras
Nicaragua
Costa rica
Panama

Caribbean Sea

SENEGAL
●Gambia
Guinea-Bissau
Guinea
Sierra Leone
Liberia

BURKINA
FASO

VENEZUELA

Guyana
Suriname
*FRENCH
GUIANA*
(FRANCE)

Côte d'Ivoire
GHANA
TOGO
BENIN

●SÃO TOMÉ
AND PRINCIPE

COLOMBIA

0°

ECUADOR

Equator

TAHITI
(FRANCE)

PERU

BRAZIL

●Equatorial
Guinea

BOLIVIA

PARAGUAY

Tropic of Capricorn

CHILE

30°S

URUGUAY

ARGENTINA

*FALKLAND ISLANDS
(ISLAS MALVINAS)*
(U.K.)

Cape Horn

60°S

Antarctic Circle

A

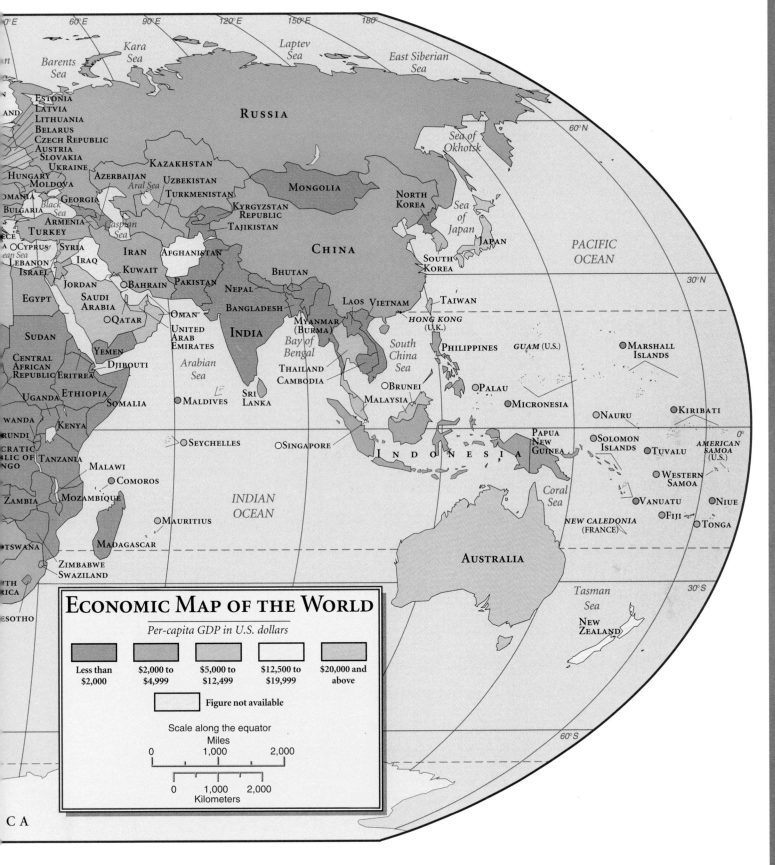

ECONOMIC MAP OF THE WORLD

Per-capita GDP in U.S. dollars

Less than $2,000	$2,000 to $4,999	$5,000 to $12,499	$12,500 to $19,999	$20,000 and above

Figure not available

Scale along the equator

Miles
0   1,000   2,000

0   1,000   2,000
Kilometers

Labels on map

Kara Sea
Barents Sea
Laptev Sea
East Siberian Sea
RUSSIA
Sea of Okhotsk
60° N
ESTONIA
LATVIA
LITHUANIA
BELARUS
CZECH REPUBLIC
AUSTRIA
SLOVAKIA
UKRAINE
HUNGARY
MOLDOVA
ROMANIA
BULGARIA
Black Sea
GEORGIA
ARMENIA
TURKEY
CYPRUS
ean Sea
LEBANON
ISRAEL
SYRIA
IRAQ
EGYPT
JORDAN
SAUDI ARABIA
KUWAIT
BAHRAIN
QATAR
OMAN
UNITED ARAB EMIRATES
YEMEN
DJIBOUTI
SUDAN
CENTRAL AFRICAN REPUBLIC
ERITREA
ETHIOPIA
UGANDA
SOMALIA
KENYA
WANDA
RUNDI
CRATIC
LIC OF
NGO
TANZANIA
MALAWI
COMOROS
ZAMBIA
MOZAMBIQUE
MAURITIUS
INDIAN OCEAN
TSWANA
ZIMBABWE
SWAZILAND
TH RICA
ESOTHO
MADAGASCAR
AZERBAIJAN
Aral Sea
Caspian Sea
KAZAKHSTAN
UZBEKISTAN
TURKMENISTAN
KYRGYZSTAN REPUBLIC
TAJIKISTAN
IRAN
AFGHANISTAN
PAKISTAN
NEPAL
BHUTAN
INDIA
BANGLADESH
MONGOLIA
CHINA
NORTH KOREA
SOUTH KOREA
Sea of Japan
JAPAN
MALDIVES
SRI LANKA
Bay of Bengal
MYANMAR (BURMA)
THAILAND
CAMBODIA
LAOS
VIETNAM
TAIWAN
HONG KONG (U.K.)
South China Sea
PHILIPPINES
Arabian Sea
SEYCHELLES
SINGAPORE
MALAYSIA
BRUNEI
INDONESIA
PALAU
MICRONESIA
PAPUA NEW GUINEA
GUAM (U.S.)
MARSHALL ISLANDS
NAURU
KIRIBATI
SOLOMON ISLANDS
TUVALU
AMERICAN SAMOA (U.S.)
WESTERN SAMOA
VANUATU
FIJI
NIUE
TONGA
NEW CALEDONIA (FRANCE)
Coral Sea
AUSTRALIA
PACIFIC OCEAN
Tasman Sea
NEW ZEALAND
30° N
0°
30° S
60° S
60° E
90° E
120° E
150° E
180°
C A

Measuring Economies

Geographers study and compare the economies of different places. One way they measure an economy is by how much industry, sometimes called industrial development, a place has. Some countries, such as Taiwan and Russia, have lots of factories to turn natural resources into manufactured goods. They are considered *industrially developed*.

Other places, such as Mexico, are considered developing countries because they have some industry but need more. Still others, such as those of Chad or Cambodia, have little industrial development. Geographers consider their natural resources under-used, or underdeveloped, in these *pre-industrial economies*.

Geographers sometimes use the term *postindustrial* to describe industrialized countries, such as the United States and Japan, that are no longer dominated by heavy industry. These postindustrial countries employ many workers to gather information, manage communications, and perform various services, such as banking or sales.

> An *economy* is the system used by a state, region, or country to manage its resources, including its money, labor, and natural and human-made materials.

The Geography of Production

Geographers look at the goods and services a country produces, including the tons of crops, the number of cars, and the number of people working in different jobs. Added together, the output of a country is called its *gross domestic product* (GDP). (See also map key pp. 82–83.)

HIGH GDPS

Countries with advanced machinery and technology:

1. Need fewer people to produce goods and supply services.
2. Create goods and provide services quickly and efficiently.

LOW GDPS

Countries without advanced machinery and technology:

1. Need more people to produce goods and supply services.
2. Create fewer goods and provide services more slowly and less efficiently.

DEVELOPMENT AND THE STANDARD OF LIVING

While GDP measures how productive a country is, geographers use another measurement when they look at how well individual people live. The *standard of living* shows how well the average person is able to find a job, a place to live, food, and an education. Generally, the more industrialized a country, the higher its standard of living. But this is not always true. For example, the standard of living in Kuwait, which has lots of oil but little other industry, is very high. On the other hand, one reason people in the former Soviet Union were dissatisfied is that they had a very low standard of living although their nation had a lot of industry.

Migration, from Exploration to Settlement

Chapter 5

An Overview of Migration

Scientists who study migration hypothesize that the first humans were born in Africa more than two million years ago and spread out from there into other parts of the world.

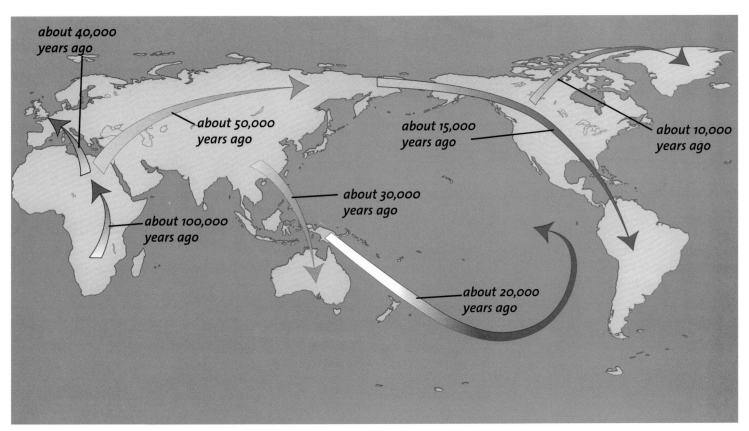

about 40,000 years ago

about 50,000 years ago

about 15,000 years ago

about 10,000 years ago

about 30,000 years ago

about 100,000 years ago

about 20,000 years ago

Many scientists and geographers believe that humans moved from Africa into Europe and Asia between 40,000 and 50,000 years ago. Then, over the next 30,000 years, they spread further to inhabit all the continents except Antarctica and many Pacific islands.

CONQUEST AND EMPIRE

In Europe in the late 1400s, an era called the **Age of Exploration** began. During this era, explorers made voyages to areas unknown to Europeans. Soon Europeans began to colonize and settle in many new places.

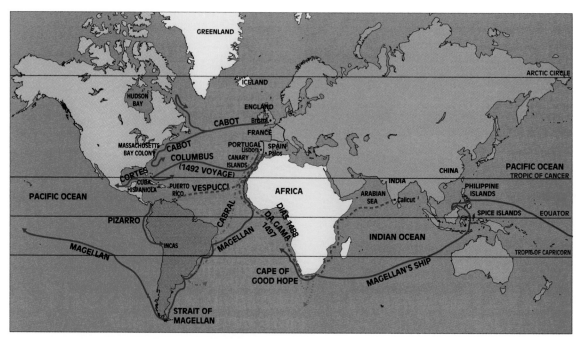

Routes of some major voyages led by European explorers.

Migration means movement from one place to settle in another. **Emigration** means movement away from one's homeland. **Immigration** means movement into a new country.

Can't Get There from Here: Transportation

In order for people to move from one region to another, they need **transportation** for themselves and their possessions. Early transportation was by foot. People simply walked from one place to another. Later, animals—horses, mules, and oxen—were tamed and used to carry passengers or packages, as well as to pull carts, sleds, and carriages.

With the Industrial Revolution (see p. 81) came the invention of machines to transport people farther in less time.

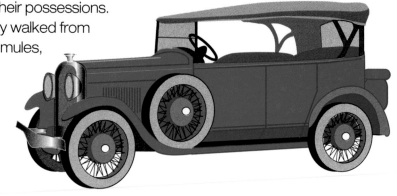

One of the products of the Industrial Revolution was the automobile.

Why Move?

People usually move from one place to another in search of a better place to live. Although there are many things that make one place better or worse than another, these things fall into two main categories:

1. Economics

2. Politics

PEOPLE MOVE AWAY FROM:	TO:	
Poverty	Areas of greater wealth	ECONOMIC REASONS
Overcrowded conditions	Greater space and comfort	
High cost of living	Affordable goods, services, and housing	
Lack of jobs	More work opportunities	ECONOMIC AND POLITICAL REASONS
Poor schools	Greater educational opportunities	
Poor health care	Available, higher-quality, health care	POLITICAL REASONS
Intolerance of race, culture, or religion	Tolerance	
Political oppression	Political choice and rights	
War or crime	Peaceful, safe life	

Appendix

Chapter 1

Glossary of Geographical Terms

acid rain

Rain that is polluted by acid in the atmosphere and damages the environment.

agriculture

Using the land to grow crops and raise animals; farming (see p. 77).

Antarctic Circle

A line of latitude that lies 66 degrees 30 minutes (66° 30′) south of the equator. From September 21 to December 21, the area north of the Antarctic Circle has daylight more than 12 hours a day. On December 21, there is daylight for 24 hours at the Antarctic Circle, then, the days get shorter until there is darkness for 24 hours on June 21.

aquifer

A layer of rock that holds water in its pores.

archipelago

A group of small islands.

Arctic Circle

A line of latitude that lies 66 degrees 30 minutes (66° 30′) north of the equator. From September 21 to December 21, the area north of the Arctic Circle is increasingly in darkness. It has 24 hours of darkness on December 21 and then daylight begins at the Arctic Circle and moves north to the pole. On March 21, the area within the Arctic Circle has 12 hours of daylight and 12 hours of darkness. From March 21 on, the hours of daylight increase until the sun shines for 24 hours on June 21.

arid

Land that is arid is extremely dry because very little rain has fallen on it.

arroyo

A dry stream bed.

arts, fine

Visual, literary, and movement arts that communicate what a culture finds beautiful.

atoll	A horseshoe-shaped island formed by coral and surrounding a lagoon.
bank, river	The land along the sides of a river or canal.
basin, river	Land drained by a river or a river system.
bay	A curved area along a coast or shore where the water juts into the land. A bay is usually smaller than a gulf and usually has a smaller opening.
bayou	A system of swampland with slow-moving streams flowing through it, found in the southern United States.
bedrock	The solid rock that lies beneath the soil on the earth's surface.
beliefs	Attitudes, ideas, and world views held by a person or group of people.
birth rate	The number of babies born alive as a proportion of the population in a specific place in a specific amount of time.
blizzard	Heavy snowfall with high wind.
bog	A small, very acidic body of water that has no natural inlets and is surrounded by rings of vegetation. A mat of grasses may grow on top. As the grasses die and build up, the bog water is replaced by a spongy mass of peat.
branch	One of the two main streams that join to form a larger river.
butte	A flat-topped hill formed when hard rock on the surface protects softer soil underneath it from being eroded. A butte is often steep-sided.
canyon	A valley with very steep sides and a flat bottom, usually cut into the rock by a river. A canyon is larger than a gorge.
cape	A point of land that extends into a sea or an ocean.
chinook	A warm, dry wind that blows down the slopes of the Rocky Mountains in winter and in early spring, and melts the snow at the base of the mountains.
city	A place where a large number of people live close together; an urban area.
cliff	A high, steep rock face.
climate	The usual weather in a particular place over a period of time.
coast	The land beside a sea or ocean.
commercial area	A part of a city where business or industry is located.

continent	A large mass of land surrounded by oceans.
continental climate	A type of climate with hot summers and cold winters, common in the center of a continent.
continental divide	A highland or ridge of mountains that causes rivers and streams to flow in different directions across continents, eventually reaching different oceans.
continental drift	The movement of the continents on the earth's surface.
continental shelf	The part of the continents that extends below sea level toward the deeper ocean.
core	The center part of the earth, consisting of a molten outer core and a solid inner core.
course, river	The part of a river between its source and its mouth.
crater	The cup-shaped indentation at the top of a volcano.
crevasse	A deep crack in a glacier.
crust	The outer layer of the earth.
cuisine	A particular style of preparing food.
culture	The behavior—language, beliefs, traditions, arts and crafts, political systems, and technologies—of a group of people.
current	Cold and warm "rivers" of seawater that flow in the oceans. Also, streams of cold or warm air that flow through the atmosphere.
customs	The traditions of a group of people.
cyclone	A name for various air movements involving spiral motion, including typhoons, hurricanes, and tornados. Also the common name for a hurricane-type storm on the Indian Ocean.
delta	An area of land shaped like a triangle where a river deposits mud, sand, or pebbles as it enters the sea.
desert	A dry region, with fewer than 10 inches of precipitation annually.
developed country	A developed country has a lot of industry and a high standard of living.
developing country	A developing country has little industry and a low standard of living.
divide	High land—either a hill or a mountain—that causes rivers to flow in different directions.

downstream	The direction of a river's flow.
downtown	The main business area of a city.
drainage	The running off of rainwater from land.
drift	Soil, silt, and rock deposited by a glacier.
drought	An extra-long period without precipitation.
drumlin	A long, narrow hill formed by glacial deposits.
dune	A hill of sand formed by blowing winds.
eclipse, lunar	Event that occurs when light from the sun is blocked by the earth passing between the sun and moon, so that the earth casts a shadow on the moon (see p. 14).
eclipse, solar	Event that occurs when sunlight is blocked by the moon as it passes between the sun and earth, casting a shadow on the earth (see p. 14).
economy	The system used by a state, region, or country to manage its industry, trade, and finance.
equator	A line on a map or globe halfway between the north and south poles. The equator is almost 25,000 miles around.
escarpment	A cliff or steep bank located inland rather than at the shore.
esker	A long, narrow ridge of coarse gravel deposited by a stream flowing under or through a glacier.
estuary	The part of a river affected by the tides of the sea into which it flows.
exurb	A sparsely populated residential area just outside the suburbs of a city.
fall line	The region where elevation drops and rivers descend over a waterfall or rapids to lower elevations.
fault	A huge crack in the earth's surface, usually caused by movement of the earth's crust.
fishery	The business of fishing; also, a fish farm.
floodplain	The low, flat area on either side of a river that the river floods in times of high water.
forest	A large, dense growth of trees, plants, and underbrush.
forestry	The process of growing, maintaining, and harvesting forests.

fork	A separation into two or more branches, as of a stream.
geographic grid	The intersecting pattern formed by lines of longitude and latitude.
geographic north pole	Also *true north pole*. The point on the earth located at 90 degrees (90°) north latitude, where the lines of longitude meet.
geography	The study of the world, how it works, and how people use and change the world as they live in it.
geopolitical	A geopolitical map shows both political and physical features.
geyser	A spout of water heated by molten rock underground.
glacier	A thick bed of ice that covers a continent or a river of thick ice that moves slowly down a slope or valley.
globe	A sphere-shaped model of the earth.
gorge	A steep-sided, V-shaped canyon, usually caused by swiftly flowing water.
gross domestic product	The total output of a country or region, including all its products and the labor of its people. (GDP)
groundwater	Water found beneath the earth's surface.
gulf	A large area of sea that is partly surrounded by land.
headwater	The source of a river or river system.
hemispheres	Halves of the earth. The equator divides the earth into northern and southern hemispheres. The prime meridian and 180 degrees (180°) longitude divide the earth into eastern and western hemispheres.
hill	A part of the earth's surface that rises gently above the level of the surrounding land.
humid	When air is humid, it contains a lot of moisture.
humus	Soil made up of decomposed animals and plants.
hurricane	A violent, usually late-summer storm in the Atlantic Ocean.
iceberg	A mass of floating ice broken off from a glacier. Only a small patch of an iceberg shows above water.
ice-cap climate	An area with an ice-cap climate is constantly covered by snow and ice.
ice floe	A sheet of floating, frozen seawater.
industry	The making and selling of products.
inland waterway	Transportation pathway by means of navigable rivers, lakes, and streams in inland areas.

international date line	A line on a map or globe drawn from the north pole to the south pole, roughly following 180 degrees (180°) longitude, but turning and twisting to miss islands and other bodies of land. It is where the days of the week change. It is one day earlier east of the date line than it is west.
island	A body of land completely surrounded by water.
isthmus	A narrow strip of land that connects two larger bodies of land.
jungle	A very dense tangle of tropical vegetation.
lagoon	A shallow body of calm water separated from the sea by a narrow strip of land.
lake	A body of water surrounded by land. The water in lakes is usually fresh, but may be salty.
landform	Any of a number of natural features on the earth's surface, including mountains, plains, plateaus, hills, canyons, cliffs, etc.
language	The use of voice sounds, gestures, and written symbols to communicate thoughts and feelings.
leeward	Facing the direction toward which the wind is blowing.
loam	Soil that contains sand and clay as well as silt and humus.
loess	Fine soil particles and dust that are carried by the wind and water and pile up to form a rich, thick soil.
magnetic north pole	The point on the earth to which a magnetized compass needle points.
mantle	The part of earth that lies between the core and the crust.
manufacturing	The creation of products from raw and recycled materials.
map	A picture of a place drawn on a flat surface.
marine climate	A mild and wet climate usually found near the sea.
marsh	A body of moving water, fresh or salty, with reeds growing in it. A marsh is usually near a river or sea coast.
megalopolis	A group of cities whose boundaries have extended to meet each other.
mental maps	Pictures in your mind of familiar places or regions.
mesa	A hill or mountain feature with a flat top and steep sides. A mesa is larger than a butte.
metropolis	A large city.
migration, human	The movement of people from one place to another, usually for economic or political reasons.

mining	Taking rocks and minerals out of the earth.
mistral	A strong, cold, dry northerly wind that sometimes brings very cold air down the Rhone River Valley in France.
monsoon	Seasonal reversal in wind direction that brings heavy rainfall in parts of southern Asia.
moraine	A mound of soil and pebbles carried by a glacier and dropped when the glacier receded.
mountain	A part of the land that rises abruptly to at least 1,000 feet above the surrounding land.
mouth, river	The place where a river flows into a larger body of water.
neighborhood	Area within a city or town that has a unique cultural makeup.
north pole	See **geographic north pole** and **magnetic north pole**.
oasis	A place in a desert where there is a source of water that can support some plant life.
ocean	A large body of saltwater that separates continents.
oxbow	A U-shaped bend in a river.
pampa	Large grassy plain of South America.
peak	The highest point of a mountain.
peninsula	A piece of land that juts into a body of water and is surrounded by water on three sides.
permafrost	Permanently frozen subsoil.
plain	Nearly flat region of land.
plate	One of the hard sections of the earth's crust on which the continents lie.
plateau	A large, mostly level area of land that stands higher than the surrounding area. A plateau is larger than a butte.
political system	Any type of government.
pond	A small body of fresh water.
population	The total number of people who live in a particular place.
population data	Facts about populations, including history, migration patterns, and cultural information.
population profile	A graph that shows different age groups within a population.
population pyramid	A bar graph that shows total population in terms of age and gender.

postindustrial economy	An economy that was once based on industry but is now based on services such as banking, computers, and health care.
prairie	Treeless plain, usually covered by tall grass.
precipitation	Any of the forms in which water falls on the earth's surface (rain, snow, hail, etc.).
pre-industrial economy	An economy with very little industry.
prevailing wind	The direction the wind usually blows across a particular place or region.
prime meridian	The line of longitude drawn from the north pole to the south pole at zero degrees (0°).
projections, map	Representations of the geographic grid used to make world maps.
rain forest	Forest in tropical climates with dense canopies, vines, and understories of growth.
range	A large area of open land. Animals usually graze on the grass on range lands.
range, mountain	A group or chain of mountains.
ravine	A deep, narrow canyon.
reef	A ridge of sand, coral, or bedrock under water but near the surface.
rift valley	A valley formed by the folding and the faulting of the earth's crust along parallel lines.
river	A large stream that flows from a source to a larger body of water, for example, a larger river, lake, sea, or ocean.
rural	A rural area is made up of farmland or countryside.
savanna	Tropical grassland with few trees.
sea	A large body of salt water surrounded partly by, or located next to land.
seamount	Underwater mountain with steep sides that rises from the ocean floor.
shore	The land beside a body of water.
silt	Fine grains of soil carried by water.
soil	Particles of bedrock, decomposed animal and plant matter, water, and air pockets that cover the earth's surface and that plants grow in.
source, river	The beginning of a river.

south pole	The point on the earth located at 90 degrees (90°) south latitude where the lines of longitude meet.
standard of living	A measurement of the availability of jobs, housing, food, and education to average citizens in a specific area or country. A high standard of living means greater availability; a low standard, lesser availability.
steppe	Any of the vast, treeless plains found in southeastern Europe and Asia.
steppe climate	Dry climate, but with greater precipitation than in a desert climate.
strait	A narrow body of water that connects two larger bodies of water.
stream	A small river.
suburb	Residential area lying just outside a city or town.
swamp	A wetland similar to a marsh but usually larger in area. It supports a wider variety of plant life, including trees and shrubs.
tableland	A plateau.
taiga	Cool, high-latitude land with low trees.
technology	The use of scientific knowledge, usually to improve industry or commerce.
tectonic plates	The pieces of the earth's crust that float on the mantle.
temperate climate	A climate without extremes of either heat or cold.
temperature	A measurement of heat.
thunderstorm	A storm accompanied by lightning, thunder, heavy rain, and sometimes hail.
tide	A change in the level of an ocean or a sea, both daily and over a year, due to the pull of gravity between the earth and the moon.
till	Soil and rock deposits spread out by a glacier as it moves or melts.
tornado	Violent and destructive cyclone that occurs inland.
trade wind	The prevailing wind of the tropics.
tributary	A stream or river that flows into a larger stream or river.
Tropic of Cancer	A line of latitude that runs parallel to the equator. It is located at 23 degrees 30 minutes (23° 30′) north of the equator. During the summer solstice (June 21), the sun is directly overhead at the Tropic of Cancer.

Tropic of Capricorn	A line of latitude that runs parallel to the equator. It is located at 23 degrees 30 minutes (23° 30′) south of the equator. During the winter solstice (December 21), the sun is directly overhead at the Tropic of Capricorn.
tsunami	A huge wave that may sometimes move through the water faster than 400 miles an hour and reach a height of more than 100 feet.
tundra	A treeless plain in the arctic where only mosses and low-growing plants can grow.
typhoon	A violent late-summer storm in the northwest Pacific.
urban	An urban area is a city or town.
valley	A U-shaped lowland between hills or mountains.
volcano	An opening in the earth's crust from which molten rocks erupt. The rocks usually form a mountain around the opening.
watershed	Area whose rainfall runs, on the surface and as groundwater, to feed a particular river.
weather	The conditions in the earth's atmosphere at a certain place and time.
weathering	The breakdown of rock on the earth's surface due to wind, water, and chemical actions.
wind	Air moving across the earth's surface.
windward	Facing the direction from which the wind is blowing.

Chapter 2 Atlas

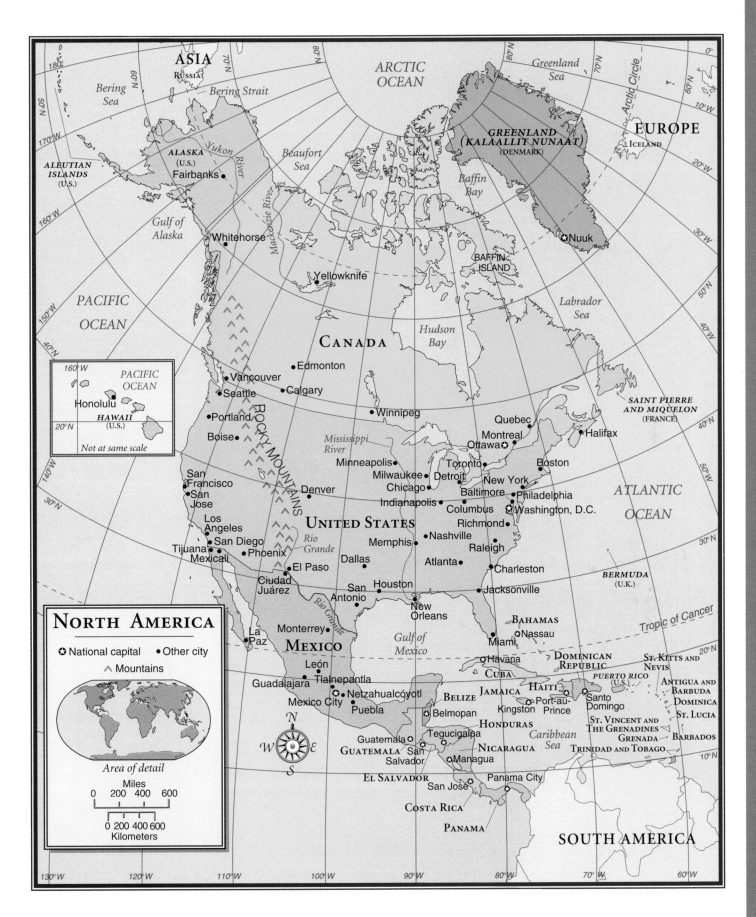

ASIA

RUSSIA

ARCTIC OCEAN

Greenland Sea

EUROPE

Bering Sea

Bering Strait

ALASKA (U.S.)

Yukon River

Fairbanks

GREENLAND (KALAALLIT NUNAAT) (DENMARK)

ICELAND

ALEUTIAN ISLANDS (U.S.)

Beaufort Sea

Gulf of Alaska

Whitehorse

Baffin Bay

PACIFIC OCEAN

Mackenzie River

Yellowknife

BAFFIN ISLAND

Nuuk

Labrador Sea

160° W

PACIFIC OCEAN

Honolulu

HAWAII (U.S.)

20° N

Not at same scale

Hudson Bay

CANADA

Edmonton

Vancouver

Calgary

Seattle

Winnipeg

Portland

Boise

ROCKY MOUNTAINS

Mississippi River

Quebec

Montreal

Ottawa

Halifax

SAINT PIERRE AND MIQUELON (FRANCE)

Minneapolis

Milwaukee

Chicago

Detroit

Toronto

Boston

New York

San Francisco

San Jose

Denver

Indianapolis

Baltimore

Philadelphia

Columbus

Washington, D.C.

ATLANTIC OCEAN

UNITED STATES

Los Angeles

San Diego

Tijuana

Phoenix

Mexicali

Rio Grande

El Paso

Richmond

Memphis

Nashville

Raleigh

Dallas

Atlanta

Charleston

BERMUDA (U.K.)

Ciudad Juárez

San Antonio

Houston

Jacksonville

Rio Grande

New Orleans

BAHAMAS

Nassau

Tropic of Cancer

NORTH AMERICA

⚙ National capital   ● Other city

⋀ Mountains

Area of detail

La Paz

Monterrey

MEXICO

Gulf of Mexico

Miami

Havana

CUBA

DOMINICAN REPUBLIC

ST. KITTS AND NEVIS

PUERTO RICO (U.S.)

ANTIGUA AND BARBUDA

León

Guadalajara

Tlalnepantla

Netzahualcóyotl

Mexico City

Puebla

BELIZE

JAMAICA

Kingston

HAITI

Port-au-Prince

Santo Domingo

DOMINICA

ST. LUCIA

Belmopan

HONDURAS

ST. VINCENT AND THE GRENADINES

GRENADA

BARBADOS

N

W   E

S

Miles

0 200 400 600

0 200 400 600

Kilometers

Guatemala

GUATEMALA

San Salvador

Tegucigalpa

NICARAGUA

Managua

Caribbean Sea

TRINIDAD AND TOBAGO

EL SALVADOR

San José

Panama City

COSTA RICA

PANAMA

SOUTH AMERICA

130° W **120° W** **110° W** **100° W** **90° W** **80° W** **70° W** **60° W**

Caribbean Sea

NORTH AMERICA

ATLANTIC
OCEAN

Maracaibo
Barranquilla
Caracas
Valencia
Cartagena
VENEZUELA
GUYANA
Georgetown
Paramaribo
Cayenne
Orinoco River
Medellín
FRENCH GUIANA
(FRANCE)
Bogotá
Cali
COLOMBIA
SURINAME

GALAPAGOS ISLANDS
(ECUADOR)
ECUADOR
Quito
Guayaquil
Manaus
Amazon River
Belém

Fortaleza

PERU
BRAZIL

Recife

Lima
Salvador

BOLIVIA
Brasília

La Paz

Sucre
Belo Horizonte

PARAGUAY
Paraná River

São Paulo
Rio de Janeiro

Asunción
Curitiba

ANDES MOUNTAINS
Pôrto Alegre

Córdoba
Valparaíso
Rosario

Santiago
URUGUAY
Montevideo

PACIFIC OCEAN
Concepción
Buenos Aires

ARGENTINA
CHILE
Puerto Montt

N
W E
S

Strait of Magellan

FALKLAND ISLANDS
(ISLAS MALVINAS)
(U.K.)
SOUTH GEORGIA ISLAND
(U.K.)

Cape Horn

SOUTH AMERICA

⊙ National capital   ● Other city

∧ Mountains

Area of detail

Miles
0   200   400   600

0   200 400 600
Kilometers

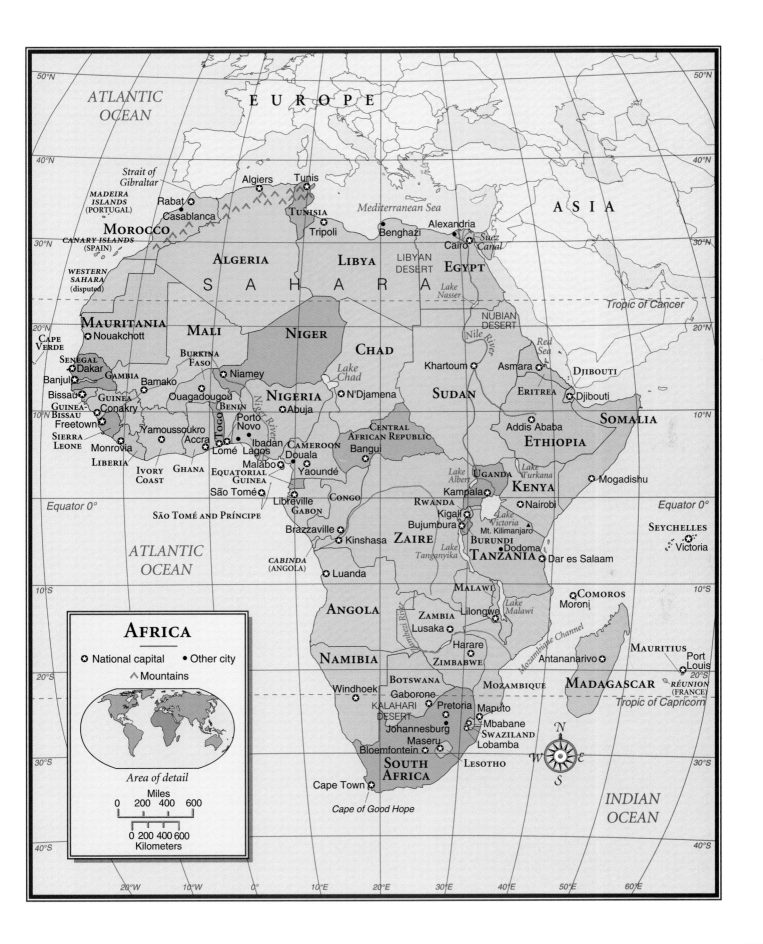

ATLANTIC
OCEAN

E U R O P E

50°N

40°N

Strait of
Gibraltar

MADEIRA
ISLANDS
(PORTUGAL)

Algiers

Tunis

Rabat
Casablanca

TUNISIA

Mediterranean Sea

A S I A

MOROCCO

Tripoli

Benghazi

Alexandria

CANARY ISLANDS
(SPAIN)

30°N

Cairo

Suez
Canal

WESTERN
SAHARA
(disputed)

ALGERIA

LIBYA

LIBYAN
DESERT

EGYPT

Lake
Nasser

Tropic of Cancer

S A H A R A

MAURITANIA

20°N

MALI

NIGER

CAPE
VERDE

Nouakchott

NUBIAN
DESERT

Nile River

20°N

CHAD

BURKINA
FASO

Niamey

SENEGAL

Banjul

Dakar

GAMBIA

Bamako

Bissau

Ouagadougou

GUINEA

Conakry

GUINEA-
BISSAU

Freetown

SIERRA
LEONE

Monrovia

BENIN

NIGERIA

Abuja

N'Djamena

Khartoum

Asmara

Red
Sea

DJIBOUTI

ERITREA

Djibouti

SUDAN

SOMALIA

10°N

Yamoussoukro

Accra

Ibadan

Lomé

Lagos

Porto
Novo

CAMEROON

Douala

CENTRAL
AFRICAN REPUBLIC

Bangui

Addis Ababa

ETHIOPIA

LIBERIA

IVORY
COAST

GHANA

EQUATORIAL
GUINEA

Malabo

Yaoundé

São Tomé

Libreville

GABON

CONGO

UGANDA

Lake
Albert

Lake
Turkana

Mogadishu

Kampala

KENYA

Equator 0°

SÃO TOMÉ AND PRÍNCIPE

RWANDA

Kigali

Lake
Victoria

Nairobi

SEYCHELLES

Equator 0°

Brazzaville

Bujumbura

Mt. Kilimanjaro

Victoria

ATLANTIC
OCEAN

Kinshasa

ZAIRE

BURUNDI

Lake
Tanganyika

Dodoma

TANZANIA

Dar es Salaam

CABINDA
(ANGOLA)

Luanda

10°S

MALAWI

COMOROS

Moroni

ANGOLA

Zambezi River

Lilongwe

Lake
Malawi

ZAMBIA

MAURITIUS

Lusaka

Port
Louis

Harare

Antananarivo

20°S

NAMIBIA

ZIMBABWE

MADAGASCAR

RÉUNION
(FRANCE)

BOTSWANA

Windhoek

Gaborone

MOZAMBIQUE

Mozambique Channel

Tropic of Capricorn

KALAHARI
DESERT

Pretoria

Maputo

Johannesburg

Mbabane

SWAZILAND

Maseru

Lobamba

Bloemfontein

LESOTHO

SOUTH
AFRICA

Cape Town

Cape of Good Hope

INDIAN
OCEAN

40°S

AFRICA

✪ National capital   • Other city

∧ Mountains

Area of detail

Miles

0   200 400 600

0 200 400 600
Kilometers

ARCTIC OCEAN

Norwegian Sea

ICELAND
⊕Reykjavík

Arctic Circle

⚘ *FAEROE ISLANDS* (DENMARK)

SHETLAND ISLANDS (U.K.)

SWEDEN

NORWAY

Gulf of Bothnia

FIN

Bergen•
Oslo⊕

Hels•

Stockholm⊕

Baltic Sea

•Göteborg

E

ATLANTIC OCEAN

North Sea

DENMARK

Riga

LITHU

RUSSIA

NORTHERN IRELAND (U.K.) *SCOTLAND*
Edinburgh•
Belfast• Glasgow•

IRELAND **UNITED KINGDOM**
Dublin⊕
Cork• •Manchester
•Birmingham
WALES *ENGLAND*
London⊕
Thames

Copenhagen⊕

•Hamburg

Elbe River

Warsaw⊕

•Berlin

POLAND

•Łódź

•Wrocław

Amsterdam•
The Hague•
BELGIUM
Brussels⊕

Rhine River

Cologne•

GERMANY

⊕Prague

CZECH REPUBLIC

Vistula River

•Kraków

English Channel

•Luxembourg
LUXEMBOURG

•Paris

LIECHTENSTEIN
Danube River

⊕Vienna

SLOVAKIA
⊕Bratislava

•Munich

AUSTRIA

⊕Budapest

Loire River
Nantes•

Seine River

Vaduz•
⊕Bern
SWITZERLAND

HUNGARY

W ⊕ E
N S

FRANCE

Bay of Biscay

Bordeaux•

Rhône River

Lyon•

ALPS

•Milan
•Turin

SLOVENIA
Ljubljana⊕ ⊕Zagreb
CROATIA

Po River

•Toulouse

Monaco•

SAN MARINO

BOSNIA AND HERZEGOVINA

Belgrad

•Porto

Marseille• **MONACO**
⊕Monaco

San Marino•

Sarajevo•

SERBIA MONTEN (YUGOSLA

ANDORRA
Andorra la Vella

PORTUGAL

Tagus River ⊕Madrid

Barcelona•

VATICAN CITY

CORSICA (FRANCE)

⊕Rome

Adriatic Sea

Lisbon⊕

SPAIN

Valencia•

•Seville

Strait of Gibraltar

BALEARIC ISLANDS (SPAIN)

SARDINIA (ITALY)

Naples•

ITALY

Tiranë⊕

ALBANIA

Sk M.

G

Tyrrhenian Sea

GIBRALTAR (U.K.)

Mediterranean Sea

Palermo•

SICILY (ITALY)

Ionian Sea

A F R I C A

Valletta⊕ **MALTA**

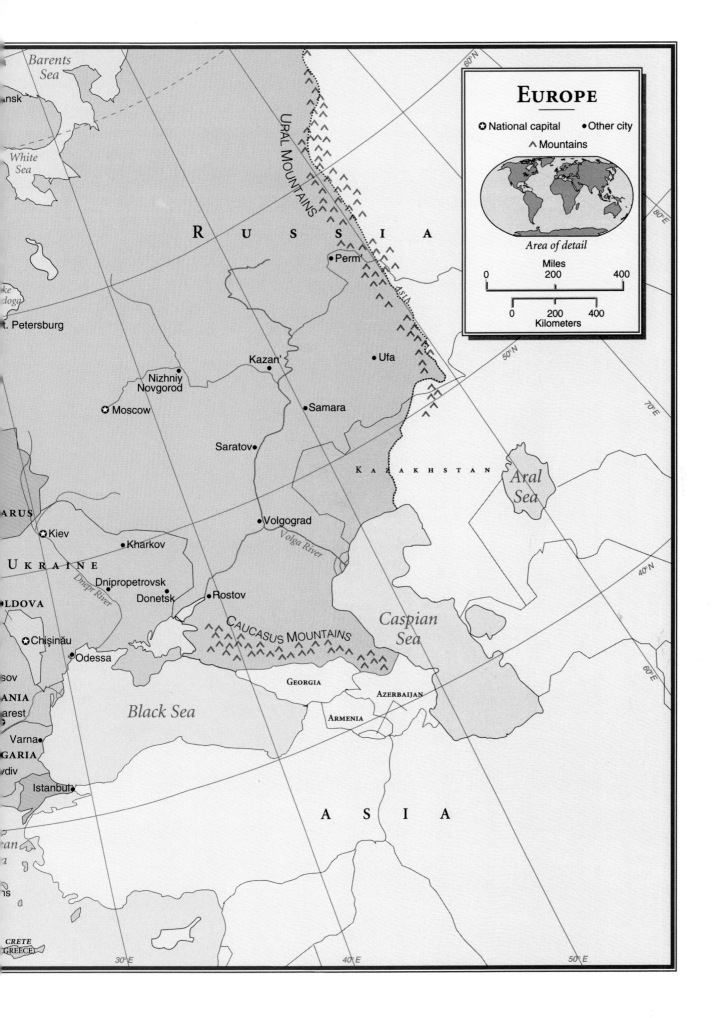

Barents
Sea

White
Sea

ansk

t. Petersburg

ke
doga

URAL MOUNTAINS

R   U   S   S   I   A

ASIA

•Perm'

•Ufa

Kazan'•

Nizhniy
Novgorod•

✪ Moscow

•Samara

Saratov•

K A Z A K H S T A N

Aral
Sea

ARUS

✪Kiev

•Kharkov

U K R A I N E

Dnepr River

Dnipropetrovsk•

Donetsk• •Rostov

•Volgograd

Volga River

LDOVA

✪Chişinău

•Odessa

sov

CAUCASUS MOUNTAINS

Caspian
Sea

ANIA
arest

Black Sea

GEORGIA

AZERBAIJAN

ARMENIA

Varna•

GARIA

vdiv

Istanbul•

A   S   I   A

an

CRETE
(GREECE)

30° E

40° E

50° E

60° N

80° E

50° N

70° E

40° N

60° E

EUROPE

✪ National capital   • Other city

⋀ Mountains

Area of detail

Miles
0   200   400

0   200   400
Kilometers

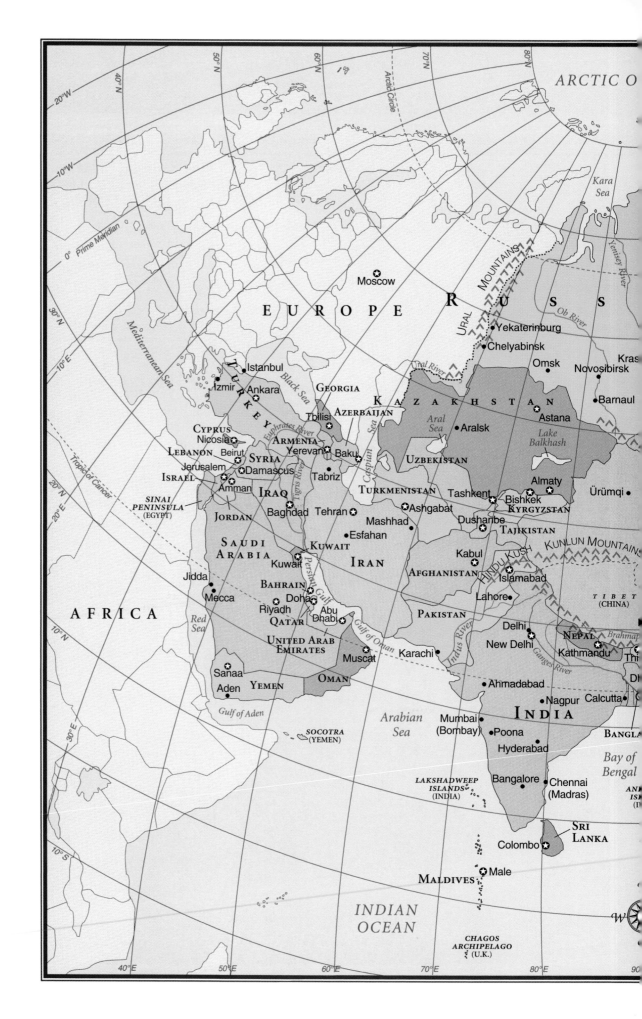

ARCTIC O

Kara Sea

Moscow

E U R O P E   R U S S

Yenisey River

URAL MOUNTAINS

Ob River

Yekaterinburg

Chelyabinsk

Omsk   Kras

Novosibirsk

Ural River

Istanbul

TURKEY   *Black Sea*   GEORGIA   K A Z A K H S T A N   Barnaul

Izmir   Ankara

Tbilisi   AZERBAIJAN   *Aral Sea*   Astana

CYPRUS   ARMENIA   Aralsk   *Lake Balkhash*

Nicosia   Yerevan   Baku

LEBANON   Beirut   UZBEKISTAN

Jerusalem   SYRIA   Almaty

ISRAEL   Damascus   Tabriz   TURKMENISTAN   Tashkent   Ürümqi

Amman   Bishkek   KYRGYZSTAN

SINAI   IRAQ   Ashgabat   Dushanbe

PENINSULA   Baghdad   Tehran   TAJIKISTAN   KUNLUN MOUNTAINS

(EGYPT)   JORDAN   Mashhad

          Esfahan   Kabul   HINDU KUSH

SAUDI   KUWAIT   AFGHANISTAN   Islamabad   T I B E T

ARABIA   Kuwait   IRAN   Lahore   (CHINA)

Jidda   *Persian Gulf*   PAKISTAN

          BAHRAIN   Delhi

Mecca   Doha   Abu   *Indus River*   New Delhi   NEPAL   *Brahmap*

AFRICA   *Red   Riyadh   Dhabi   Kathmandu*

          Sea*   QATAR   *Gulf of Oman*   Karachi   Th

          UNITED ARAB   Muscat   Dh

          EMIRATES   OMAN   Ahmadabad

Sanaa   *Ganges River*

Aden   YEMEN   Nagpur   Calcutta

Gulf of Aden   Mumbai   I N D I A   BANGLA

          *Arabian   (Bombay)   Poona

          Sea*   Hyderabad

*LAKSHADWEEP   Bangalore   *Bay of*

ISLANDS   Chennai   Bengal*

(INDIA)   (Madras)   AN

                    ISL

                    (I

               SRI

               LANKA

          Colombo

          Male

MALDIVES

I N D I A N

OCEAN   W

*CHAGOS
ARCHIPELAGO
(U.K.)*

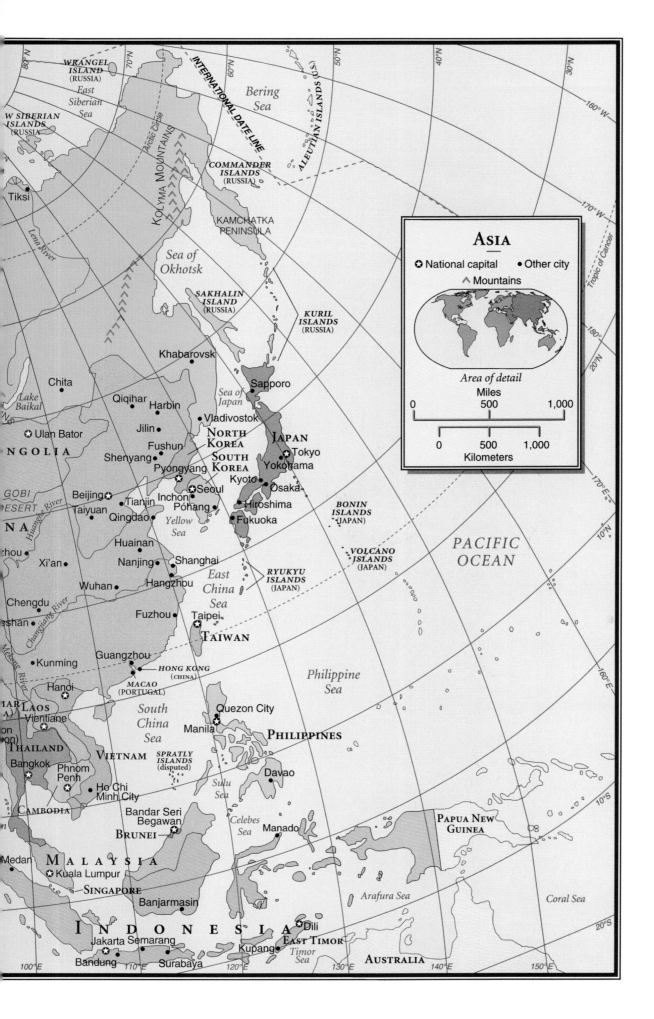

WRANGEL
ISLAND
(RUSSIA)

East
Siberian
Sea

W SIBERIAN
ISLANDS
(RUSSIA)

INTERNATIONAL DATE LINE

Bering
Sea

ALEUTIAN ISLANDS (U.S.)

Arctic Circle

Tiksi

KOLYMA MOUNTAINS

Lena River

COMMANDER
ISLANDS
(RUSSIA)

KAMCHATKA
PENINSULA

Sea of
Okhotsk

SAKHALIN
ISLAND
(RUSSIA)

KURIL
ISLANDS
(RUSSIA)

Khabarovsk

Chita

Lake
Baikal

Qiqihar

Harbin

Sapporo

Sea of
Japan

Vladivostok

Jilin

Ulan Bator

NGOLIA

Fushun

NORTH
KOREA

JAPAN

Shenyang

SOUTH
KOREA

Tokyo

Pyongyang

Yokohama

GOBI
DESERT

Beijing

Tianjin

Seoul

Kyoto

Osaka

Taiyuan

Inchon

Pohang

Hiroshima

NA

Qingdao

Yellow
Sea

Fukuoka

BONIN
ISLANDS
(JAPAN)

Huainan

zhou

Xi'an

Nanjing

Shanghai

East
China
Sea

RYUKYU
ISLANDS
(JAPAN)

PACIFIC
OCEAN

VOLCANO
ISLANDS
(JAPAN)

Wuhan

Hangzhou

Changjiang River

Chengdu

eshan

Mekong River

Fuzhou

Taipei

Kunming

Guangzhou

HONG KONG
(CHINA)

TAIWAN

MACAO
(PORTUGAL)

Hanoi

South
China
Sea

Philippine
Sea

AR

LAOS

Vientiane

on)

Quezon City

Manila

PHILIPPINES

THAILAND

VIETNAM

SPRATLY
ISLANDS
(disputed)

Bangkok

Phnom
Penh

Ho Chi
Minh City

Davao

CAMBODIA

Bandar Seri
Begawan

Sulu
Sea

Celebes
Sea

Manado

PAPUA NEW
GUINEA

BRUNEI

Medan

MALAYSIA

Kuala Lumpur

SINGAPORE

Arafura Sea

Coral Sea

Banjarmasin

I N D O N E S I A

Dili

Jakarta

Semarang

EAST TIMOR

Kupang

Timor
Sea

Bandung

Surabaya

AUSTRALIA

ASIA

⊕ National capital • Other city

⋀ Mountains

Area of detail

Miles

0   500   1,000

0   500   1,000

Kilometers

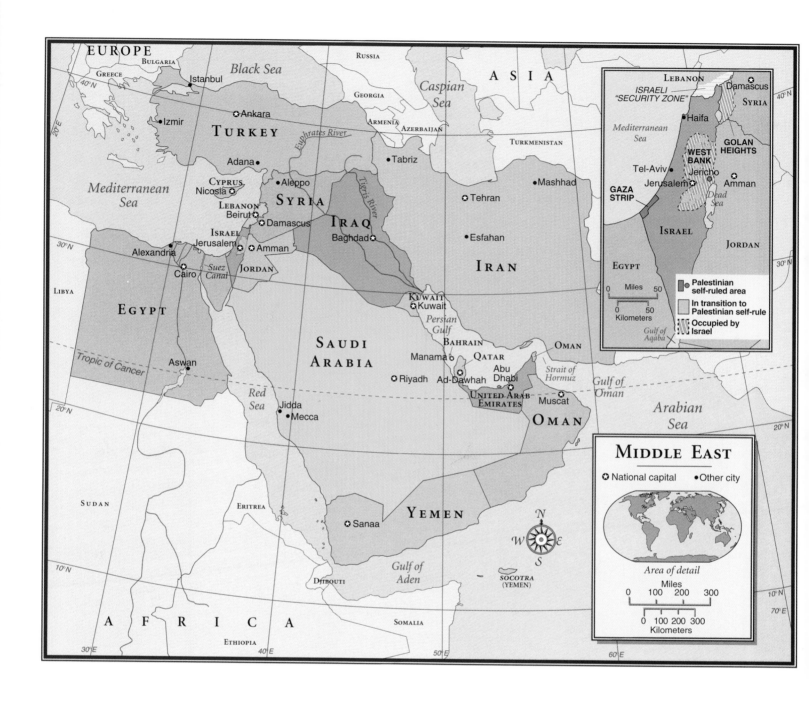

EUROPE

GREECE
BULGARIA
Istanbul
Izmir
Ankara
Black Sea
RUSSIA
GEORGIA
Caspian Sea
ARMENIA
AZERBAIJAN
TURKMENISTAN
ASIA

TURKEY
Adana
Euphrates River
Tabriz
Mashhad

Mediterranean Sea
CYPRUS
Nicosia
Aleppo
SYRIA
Tigris River
Tehran
LEBANON
Beirut
Damascus
IRAQ
Baghdad
Esfahan

ISRAEL
Jerusalem
Amman
JORDAN
IRAN

LIBYA
Alexandria
Cairo
Suez Canal
Kuwait
Kuwait
Persian Gulf
BAHRAIN
Manama
QATAR
Abu Dhabi
OMAN
Strait of Hormuz
Gulf of Oman

EGYPT

SAUDI ARABIA
Tropic of Cancer
Aswan
Riyadh
Ad-Dawhah
UNITED ARAB EMIRATES
Muscat
OMAN
Arabian Sea

Red Sea
Jidda
Mecca

SUDAN
ERITREA
YEMEN
Sanaa
Gulf of Aden

AFRICA
DJIBOUTI
SOCOTRA (YEMEN)
SOMALIA
ETHIOPIA

Inset (top right):

LEBANON
ISRAELI "SECURITY ZONE"
Damascus
SYRIA
Mediterranean Sea
Haifa
GOLAN HEIGHTS
Tel-Aviv
WEST BANK
Jerusalem
Jericho
Amman
GAZA STRIP
Dead Sea
Israel
JORDAN
EGYPT
Gulf of Aqaba

0   Miles   50
0   50
Kilometers

● Palestinian self-ruled area
☐ In transition to Palestinian self-rule
▨ Occupied by Israel

Inset (bottom right):

MIDDLE EAST

✪ National capital   ● Other city

Area of detail

Miles
0 100 200 300

0 100 200 300
Kilometers

106

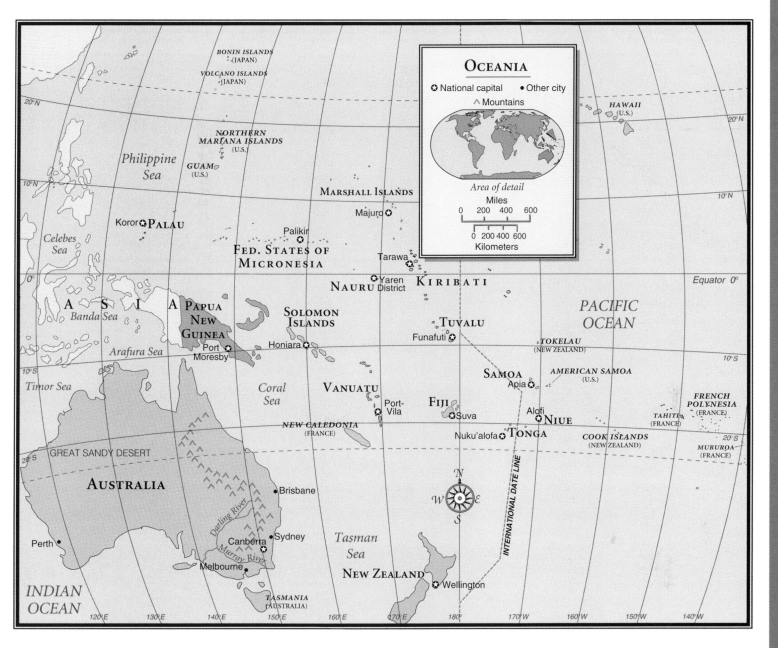

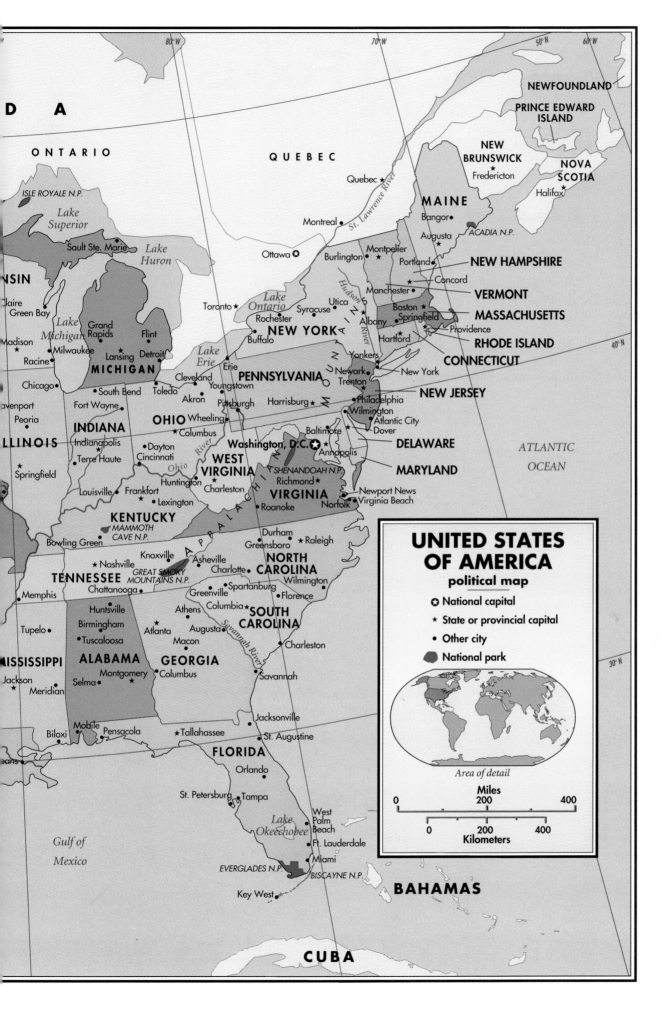

CANADA

ONTARIO

QUEBEC

NEWFOUNDLAND

PRINCE EDWARD ISLAND

NEW BRUNSWICK
★ Fredericton

NOVA SCOTIA
Halifax ★

ISLE ROYALE N.P.

Lake Superior

Sault Ste. Marie

Lake Huron

Quebec ★

Montreal ●

St. Lawrence River

Ottawa ✪

MAINE
Bangor ●
Augusta ★

ACADIA N.P.

WISCONSIN
Eau Claire
Green Bay

Lake Michigan

Madison
Milwaukee ●
Racine ●

Grand Rapids ●
Flint ●
Lansing ★
Detroit ●

MICHIGAN

Burlington ●

Toronto ★

Lake Ontario

Rochester ●
Syracuse ●
Utica ●

NEW YORK

Buffalo ●

Montpelier ★

Manchester ●

Albany ★

Hudson River

Portland ●

NEW HAMPSHIRE
Concord ★

VERMONT

Boston ★
Springfield ●

MASSACHUSETTS

Providence ★

Hartford ★

RHODE ISLAND

CONNECTICUT

Chicago ●
South Bend ●
Toledo ●
Fort Wayne ●

Cleveland ●
Youngstown ●
Akron ●
Erie ●

Lake Erie

PENNSYLVANIA

Pittsburgh ●
Harrisburg ★

Yonkers ●
Newark ●
Trenton ★

New York ●

NEW JERSEY

Davenport ●
Peoria ●

INDIANA

ILLINOIS

Indianapolis ★
Terre Haute ●

Springfield ★

OHIO
Wheeling ●
Columbus ★

Dayton ●
Cincinnati ●

Ohio River

WEST VIRGINIA

Philadelphia ●
Wilmington ●
Atlantic City ●
Dover ★

DELAWARE

Washington, D.C. ✪
Annapolis ★

ATLANTIC OCEAN

Louisville ●
Frankfort ★
Lexington ●

Huntington ●
Charleston ★

SHENANDOAH N.P.
Richmond ★

Baltimore ●

MARYLAND

KENTUCKY

MAMMOTH CAVE N.P.

Bowling Green ●

VIRGINIA

Roanoke ●

Newport News ●
Virginia Beach ●
Norfolk ●

APPALACHIAN MTS.

Durham ●
Greensboro ●
Raleigh ●

Nashville ★
Knoxville ●
Asheville ●

GREAT SMOKY MOUNTAINS N.P.

Chattanooga ●

TENNESSEE

Memphis ●

Charlotte ●

NORTH CAROLINA

Wilmington ●

Greenville ●
Spartanburg ●
Florence ●

Athens ●
Columbia ★

SOUTH CAROLINA

Huntsville ●

Birmingham ●
Tuscaloosa ●

Atlanta ★
Macon ●

Augusta ●

Savannah River

Charleston ●

Tupelo ●

MISSISSIPPI

Jackson ★
Meridian ●

ALABAMA

Selma ●
Montgomery ★

Columbus ●

GEORGIA

Savannah ●

Biloxi ●
Mobile ●
Pensacola ●

New Orleans

Tallahassee ★

Jacksonville ●

St. Augustine ●

FLORIDA

Orlando ●

St. Petersburg ●
Tampa ●

Lake Okeechobee

West Palm Beach ●

Ft. Lauderdale ●

EVERGLADES N.P.
Miami ●
BISCAYNE N.P.

Gulf of Mexico

Key West ●

BAHAMAS

CUBA

UNITED STATES OF AMERICA
political map

✪ National capital
★ State or provincial capital
● Other city
⬤ National park

Area of detail

Miles
0   200   400

Kilometers
0   200   400

80° W   70° W   50° N   60° W

40° N

30° N

Chapter 3

The World in Focus

COUNTRY	CAPITAL	AREA SQ MI	AREA SQ KM	POPULATION	LANGUAGE	RELIGION	CURRENCY	GOVERNMENT
AFGHANISTAN	Kabul	251,825	652,227	25,824,882	Pashto	Sunni Muslim	Afghani	Transitional administration
ALBANIA	Tiranë	11,100	28,749	3,364,571	Albanian	Muslim	Lek	Republic
ALGERIA	Algiers	919,595	2,381,751	31,133,486	Arabic	Sunni Muslim	Dinar	Republic
ANDORRA	Andorra la Vella	181	469	65,939	Catalan	Catholic	Euro	Parliamentary co-principality
ANGOLA	Luanda	481,351	1,246,699	11,177,537	Portuguese/ Umbundu	Catholic/ Traditional beliefs	Kwanza	Republic
ANTIGUA & BARBUDA	St. John's	170	440	64,246	English	Anglican	East Caribbean Dollar	Constitutional monarchy with British-style parliament
ARGENTINA	Buenos Aires	1,057,518	2,738,972	37,737,664	Spanish	Catholic	Peso	Republic
ARMENIA	Yerevan	11,506	29,801	3,409,234	Armenian	Armenian Apostolic	Dram	Republic
AUSTRALIA	Canberra	2,967,893	7,686,843	18,783,551	English	Catholic/Anglican	Australian Dollar	Democratic, federal state system
AUSTRIA	Vienna	32,374	83,849	8,139,299	German	Catholic	Euro	Parliamentary democracy
AZERBAIJAN	Baku	33,436	86,599	7,908,224	Azeri	Shia Muslim	Manat	Republic
BAHAMAS	Nassau	5,382	13,939	283,705	English	Baptist/ Nonreligious/ Catholic	U.S. Dollar	Independent commonwealth
BAHRAIN	Manama	268	694	629,090	Arabic	Shia Muslim	Dinar	Traditional monarchy
BANGLADESH	Dhaka	55,598	143,999	127,117,967	Bengali	Sunni Muslim	Taka	Parliamentary democracy
BARBADOS	Bridgetown	166	430	259,191	English	Anglican/Pentecostal	Dollar	Parliamentary democracy
BELARUS	Minsk	80,154	207,599	10,401,784	Belorussian/ Russian	Nonreligious/ Orthodox	Ruble	Republic
BELGIUM	Brussels	11,780	30,510	10,182,034	Flemish/French	Catholic	Euro	Parliamentary democracy under a constitutional monarch
BELIZE	Belmopan	8,865	22,960	235,789	English/Creole	Catholic	Belize Dollar	Parliamentary democracy
BENIN	Porto Novo	43,483	112,621	6,305,567	Fon	Indigenous beliefs	CFA Franc	Republic
BHUTAN	Thimphu	18,417	47,000	1,951,965	Dzonghka	Lamaistic Buddhist	Ngultrum	Monarchy
BOLIVIA	La Paz; Sucre	424,162	1,098,580	7,982,850	Spanish/ Quechua/Aymara	Catholic	Boliviano	Republic

COUNTRY	CAPITAL	AREA SQ MI	AREA SQ KM	POPULATION	LANGUAGE	RELIGION	CURRENCY	GOVERNMENT
BOSNIA-HERZEGOVINA	Sarajevo	19,781	51,233	3,370,000	Serb/Croat	Sunni Muslim/ Serbian Orthodox/ Catholic	Marka	Republic
BOTSWANA	Gaborone	275,000	712,250	1,464,167	English/Tswana	Traditional beliefs/ African churches	Pula	Parliamentary republic
BRAZIL	Brasília	3,286,470	8,511,957	171,853,126	Portuguese	Catholic	Real	Federal republic
BRUNEI	Bandar Seri Begawan	2,228	5,771	322,982	Malay	Sunni Muslim	Bruneian Dollar	Independent sultanate
BULGARIA	Sofia	42,822	110,909	8,194,772	Bulgarian	Nonreligious	Lev	Republic
BURKINA FASO	Ouagadougou	105,869	274,201	11,575,898	Mossi	Muslim	CFA Franc	Republic
BURUNDI	Bujumbura	10,745	27,830	5,735,937	Rundi	Catholic	Franc	In transition
CAMBODIA	Phnom Penh	69,900	181,041	11,626,520	Khmer	Therevada Buddhist	Riel	Constitutional monarchy
CAMEROON	Yaoundé	183,567	475,439	15,456,092	Fang/Murri/ French	Catholic/ Traditional beliefs	CFA Franc	Republic
CANADA	Ottawa	3,851,800	9,976,162	31,006,347	English/French	Catholic/ Protestant	Canadian Dollar	Confederation with parliamentary democracy
CAPE VERDE	Praia	1,556	4,030	405,748	Creole/ Portuguese	Catholic	Escudo	Republic
CENTRAL AFRICAN REPUBLIC	Bangui	240,533	622,980	3,444,951	Sango/French	Traditional beliefs/ Baptist/Catholic	CFA Franc	Republic
CHAD	N'Djamena	495,752	1,283,998	7,557,436	Sara	Sunni Muslim	CFA Franc	Republic
CHILE	Santiago	292,258	756,948	14,973,843	Spanish	Catholic	Peso	Republic
CHINA, PEOPLE'S REPUBLIC OF	Beijing	3,696,527	9,573,998	1,250,066,000	Mandarin Chinese	Atheist	Yuan	Communist party–led state
COLOMBIA	Bogotá	440,762	1,141,574	39,309,422	Spanish	Catholic	Peso	Republic
COMORO ISLANDS	Moroni	719	1,862	562,723	Arabic	Sunni Muslim	Franc	In transition
CONGO, REPUBLIC OF	Brazzaville	132,046	341,999	2,716,814	French/ Monokutuba	Catholic	CFA Franc	Republic
COSTA RICA	San José	19,730	51,101	3,674,490	Spanish	Catholic	Colon	Republic
CROATIA	Zagreb	21,829	56,537	4,676,865	Croatian	Catholic	Kuna	Parliamentary democracy
CUBA	Havana	42,803	110,860	11,096,395	Spanish	Nonreligious	Cuban Peso	Communist state
CYPRUS	Nicosia	3,571	9,249	754,064	Greek/Turkish	Greek Orthodox/ Sunni Muslim	Pound	Republic
CZECH REPUBLIC	Prague	30,387	78,702	10,281,513	Czech	Catholic	Koruna	Republic
DEMOCRATIC REPULIC OF CONGO	Kinshasa	905,563	2,345,408	50,481,305	French/Lingala	Catholic	Congolese Franc	Republic with strong presidential authority (in transition)
DENMARK	Copenhagen	16,639	43,095	5,356,845	Danish	Evangelical/ Lutheran	Krone	Constitutional monarchy
DJIBOUTI	Djibouti	8,494	21,999	447,439	French	Muslim	Franc	Republic
DOMINICA	Roseau	290	751	64,881	French Creole/ English	Catholic	East Caribbean Dollar	Parliamentary democracy
DOMINICAN REPUBLIC	Santo Domingo	18,815	48,731	8,129,734	Spanish	Catholic	Peso	Republic
EAST TIMOR	Dili	5,743	14,874	845,000	Tetum	Catholic	Escudo	Republic
ECUADOR	Quito	105,037	272,046	12,562,496	Spanish	Catholic	U.S. Dollar	Republic

COUNTRY	CAPITAL	AREA SQ MI	AREA SQ KM	POPULATION	LANGUAGE	RELIGION	CURRENCY	GOVERNMENT
EGYPT	Cairo	385,299	997,743	67,273,906	Arabic	Sunni Muslim	Pound	Republic
EL SALVADOR	San Salvador	13,176,59	34,125	5,839,079	Spanish	Catholic	Colón	Republic
EQUATORIAL GUINEA	Malabo	10,830	28,050	465,746	Fang/Spanish	Catholic	CFA Franc	Republic
ERITREA	Asmara	46,842	121,321	3,984,723	Tigrinya	Sunni Muslim	Nafka	In transition
ESTONIA	Tallinn	17,462	45,227	1,408,523	Estonian	Lutheran/ Nonreligious/ Estonian Orthodox	Kroon	Republic
ETHIOPIA	Addis Ababa	435,184	1,127,127	58,680,383	Amharic/Oromo	Ethiopian Orthodox/Sunni Muslim	Birr	Federal republic
FIJI	Suva	7,054	18,270	812,918	Fijian/English/ Hindi	Hindu/Methodist	Fijian Dollar	In transition
FINLAND	Helsinki	130,127	337,029	5,518,372	Finnish	Evangelical/ Lutheran	Euro	Constitutional republic
FRANCE	Paris	211,208	547,029	58,978,172	French	Catholic	Euro	Republic
GABON	Libreville	103,347	267,669	1,225,853	French/Fang	Christian/ Indigenous beliefs	CFA Franc	Republic
GAMBIA	Banjul	4,363	11,300	1,336,320	Malinke	Muslim	Dalasi	Republic
GEORGIA	Tbilisi	26,911	69,911	5,066,499	Georgian	Georgian Orthodox	Lavi	Republic
GERMANY	Berlin	137,803	356,910	83,087,361	German	Protestant/ Catholic	Euro	Federal republic
GHANA	Accra	92,100	238,539	18,887,626	Hausa	Indigenous beliefs	Cedi	Republic
GREECE	Athens	50,942	131,940	10,707,135	Greek	Greek Orthodox	Euro	Parliamentary democracy
GRENADA	St. George's	131	339	97,008	English	Catholic	East Caribbean Dollar	Parliamentary democracy
GUATEMALA	Guatemala City	42,042	108,889	12,335,580	Spanish	Catholic	Quetzal	Republic
GUINEA	Conakry	94,927	245,861	7,538,953	Fulani	Nyskun	Franc	Republic
GUINEA-BISSAU	Bissau	13,946	36,120	1,234,555	Portuguese	Indigenous beliefs	CFA Franc	Republic
GUYANA	Georgetown	83,000	214,970	705,156	English/Creole	Hindu/ Protestant	Guyanese Dollar	Republic
HAITI	Port-au-Prince	10,714	27,749	6,884,264	Haitian Creole	Catholic/Voodoo	Gourde	Republic
HONDURAS	Tegucigalpa	43,278	112,090	5,997,327	Spanish	Catholic	Lempira	Republic
HUNGARY	Budapest	35,919	93,030	10,186,372	Hungarian	Catholic	Forint	Parliamentary democracy
ICELAND	Reykjavik	36,699	1,022,819	272,512	Icelandic	Evangelical/ Lutheran	Krona	Constitutional republic
INDIA	New Delhi	1,222,243	3,165,609	1,000,848,550	Hindi	Hindu	Rupee	Federal republic
INDONESIA	Jakarta	735,309	1,904,450	202,110,000	Bahasa Indonesia	Sunni Muslim	Rupiah	Republic
IRAN	Tehran	632,457	1,638,064	65,179,752	Farsi	Shia Muslim	Rial	Islamic republic
IRAQ	Baghdad	167,975	435,055	22,427,150	Arabic	Shia Muslim	Dinar	Republic
ISRAEL	Jerusalem	7,876	20,400	5,749,760	Hebrew	Jewish	New Shekel	Republic
ITALY	Rome	116,305	301,230	56,735,130	Italian	Catholic	Euro	Republic
IVORY COAST	Yamoussoukro	124,502	322,460	15,818,068	French	Muslim	CFA Franc	Republic

COUNTRY	CAPITAL	AREA SQ MI	AREA SQ KM	POPULATION	LANGUAGE	RELIGION	CURRENCY	GOVERNMENT
JAMAICA	Kingston	4,243	10,989	2,653,443	English	Pentecostal/ Nonreligious/ Catholic	Jamaican Dollar	Parliamentary democracy
JAPAN	Tokyo	145,882	377,834	126,182,077	Japanese	Buddhist/Shinto	Yen	Constitutional monarchy
JORDAN	Amman	34,445	89,213	4,561,147	Arabic	Simmo Muslim	Dinar	Republic
KAZAKHSTAN	Astana	1,052,100	2,724,939	16,824,825	Kazakh/ Russian	Sunni Muslim/ Nonreligious	Tenge	Republic
KENYA	Nairobi	224,961	582,649	28,808,658	Swahili	Catholic/Protestant/ Traditional beliefs	Shilling	Republic
KIRIBATI	Tarawa	313	811	83,976	English/Kiribati	Catholic	Australian Dollar	Republic
KOREA, NORTH	Pyongyang	46,540	120,539	21,386,109	Korean	Nonreligious	Won	Communist state
KOREA, SOUTH	Seoul	38,023	98,480	47,884,800	Korean	Nonreligious	Won	Republic with power centralized in a strong executive
KUWAIT	Kuwait	6,880	17,819	1,991,115	Arabic	Sunni Muslim	Dinar	Constitutional monarchy
KYRGYZSTAN	Bishkek	76,641	198,500	4,546,055	Kyrgyz/Russian	Sunni Muslim	Som	Republic
LAOS	Vientiane	91,428	236,799	5,407,453	Lao	Buddhist	Kip	Communist
LATVIA	Riga	24,749	64,100	2,353,874	Latvian/ Russian	Lutheran/ Nonreligious	Lat	Republic
LEBANON	Beirut	4,015	10,399	3,562,699	Arabic	Muslim	Pound	Republic
LESOTHO	Maseru	11,718	30,350	2,128,950	Sesotho	Catholic/ Traditional beliefs	Loti	Modified constitutional monarchy
LIBERIA	Monrovia	38,520	99,068	2,923,725	Creole	Traditional	Liberian Dollar	Republic
LIBYA	Tripoli	679,358	1,759,537	4,992,838	Arabic	Sunni Muslim	Dinar	Islamic Arabic socialist "Mass-State"
LIECHTENSTEIN	Vaduz	62	161	32,057	German	Catholic	Swiss Franc	Hereditary constitutional monarchy
LITHUANIA	Vilnius	25,174	65,201	3,584,966	Lithuanian	Catholic	Litas	Republic
LUXEMBOURG	Luxembourg	999	2,587	429,080	French	Catholic	Euro	Constitutional monarchy
MACEDONIA	Skopje	9,871	25,333	2,022,604	Macedonian	Macedonian Orthodox	Denar	Republic
MADAGASCAR	Antananarivo	226,656	587,039	147,873,387	Malagasy	Indigenous beliefs	Franc	Republic
MALAWI	Lilongwe	45,745	118,480	10,000,416	English/ Chichewa	Sunni Muslim/ Catholic/Traditional beliefs	Kwacha	Multiparty democracy
MALAYSIA	Kuala Lumpur	127,316	329,748	20,932,901	Malay	Sunni Muslim	Ringgit	Federal parliamentary democracy with constitutional monarch
MALDIVES, REPUBLIC OF	Male	116	300	300,220	Divehi	Sunni Muslim	Rufiyaa	Republic
MALI	Bamako	428,077	1,108,719	10,429,124	Babara	Muslim	CFA Franc	Republic
MALTA	Valletta	124	321	381,603	Maltese/ English	Catholic	Lira	Parliamentary democracy
MARSHALL ISLANDS	Majuro	70	181	63,031	Marshallese/ English	Congregational/ Nonreligious/Catholic	U.S. Dollar	Republic

COUNTRY	CAPITAL	AREA SQ MI	AREA SQ KM	POPULATION	LANGUAGE	RELIGION	CURRENCY	GOVERNMENT
MAURITANIA	Nouakchott	397,953	1,030,698	2,581,738	Arabic	Muslim	Ouguiya	Islamic republic
MAURITIUS	Port Louis	788	2,041	1,182,212	English	Hindu	Rupee	Republic
MEXICO	Mexico City	756,066	1,958,211	100,294,036	Spanish	Catholic	New Peso	Federal republic
MICRONESIA, FEDERATED STATES OF	Palikir	271	702	129,658	English/ Chuukese	Catholic/ Congregational	U.S. Dollar	Republic
MOLDOVA	Chisinau	13,012	33,701	4,460,838	Moldovian	Nonreligious/ Romanian Orthodox	Leu	Republic
MONACO	Monaco	1	2	32,149	French	Catholic	Euro	Constitutional monarchy
MONGOLIA	Ulaanbaatar	604,247	1,565,000	2,617,379	Khalka Mongol	Tibetan Buddhist	Tugrik	Republic
MOROCCO	Rabat	177,117	458,733	29,661,636	Arabic	Sunni Muslim	Dirham	Constitutional monarchy
MOZAMBIQUE	Maputo	309,494	801,589	19,124,335	Portuguese/ Makua	Indigenous beliefs	Metical	Republic
MYANMAR	Yangon	261,969	678,500	48,081,302	Burmese	Buddhist	Kyat	Military regime
NAMIBIA	Windhoek	318,694	825,417	1,648,270	Ovambo/ English	Lutheran	Rand	Republic
NAURU	Yaren District	21	54	10,501	Nauruan	Congregational	Australian Dollar	Republic
NEPAL	Kathmandu	56,827	147,182	24,302,653	Nepali	Hindu	Rupee	Constitutional monarchy
NETHERLANDS	Amsterdam	16,033	41,525	15,807,641	Dutch	Catholic	Euro	Parliamentary democracy under a constitutional monarch
NEW ZEALAND	Wellington	107,737	279,039	3,662,265	English	Nonreligious/ Anglican/ Presbyterian	New Zealand Dollar	Parliamentary democracy
NICARAGUA	Managua	50,893	131,813	4,717,132	Spanish	Catholic	Córdoba	Republic
NIGER	Niamey	496,90	1,286,971	9,962,242	Hausa	Muslim	CFA Franc	Republic
NIGERIA	Abuja	356,668	923,770	113,828,587	Hausa	Muslim	Naira	Republic in transition from military to civilian rule
NORWAY	Oslo	125,181	324,219	4,438,547	Norwegian	Evangelical/ Lutheran	Krone	Hereditary constitutional monarchy
OMAN	Muscat	118,150	306,009	2,446,645	Arabic	Ibadhi Muslim	Rial Omani	Absolute monarchy
PAKISTAN	Islamabad	307,374	796,099	138,123,359	Urdu	Sunni Muslim	Rupee	In transition
PALAU	Koror	188	487	18,110	Palauan/ English	Catholic/ Traditional beliefs	U.S. Dollar	Republic
PANAMA	Panama City	30,193	78,200	2,778,536	Spanish	Catholic	Balboa/ U.S. Dollar	Constitutional republic
PAPUA NEW GUINEA	Port Moresby	178,793	462,841	4,599,785	Pidgin English/ English	Catholic/Lutheran	Kina	Parliamentary democracy
PARAGUAY	Asunción	157,046	406,749	5,434,095	Spanish/Guarani	Catholic	Guarani	Republic
PERU	Lima	496,223	1,285,218	26,624,582	Spanish	Catholic	New Sol	Republic
PHILIPPINES	Manila	115,830	300,000	79,345,812	Filipino	Catholic	Peso	Republic
POLAND	Warsaw	120,727	312,683	38,608,929	Polish	Catholic	Zloty	Republic
PORTUGAL	Lisbon	35,672	92,930	9,918,040	Portuguese	Catholic	Euro	Republic
QATAR	Dawhah	4,416	11,437	723,542	Arabic	Sunni Muslim	Riyal	Traditional monarchy
REPUBLIC OF IRELAND	Dublin	26,600	70,820	3,632,944	English	Catholic	Euro	Parliamentary republic

COUNTRY	CAPITAL	AREA SQ MI	AREA SQ KM	POPULATION	LANGUAGE	RELIGION	CURRENCY	GOVERNMENT
ROMANIA	Bucharest	591,699	237,423	22,334,312	Romanian	Romanian Orthodox	Leu	Republic
RUSSIAN FEDERATION	Moscow	6,592,800	17,075,352	146,393,569	Russian	Russian Orthodox	Ruble	Federal republic
RWANDA	Kigali	10,170	26,340	8,154,933	Rwanda	Catholic	Franc	Republic
ST. KITTS-NEVIS	Basseterre	104	269	42,838	English	Anglican/Methodist	East Caribbean Dollar	Constitutional monarchy
ST. LUCIA	Castries	239	619	154,020	English/French	Catholic	East Caribbean Dollar	Parliamentary democracy
ST. VINCENT AND THE GRENADINES	Kingstown	150	389	120,519	Creole	Nonreligious/ Anglican	East Caribbean Dollar	Constitutional monarchy
SAMOA	Apia	1,104	2,859	224,713	English	Mormon/ Congregational	Tala	Constitutional monarchy
SAN MARINO	San Marino	23	60	25,061	Samoan	Catholic	Euro	Republic
SÃO TOMÉ & PRÍNCIPE	São Tomé	371	961	154,878	Italian/ Portuguese	Catholic	Dobra	Republic
SAUDI ARABIA	Riyadh	864,000	2,240,350	21,504,613	Arabic	Sunni Muslim	Riyal	Monarchy with council of ministers
SENEGAL	Dakar	75,749	197,190	10,051,930	Wolof	Muslim	CFA Franc	Republic
SERBIA AND MONTENEGRO	Belgrade	35,517	102,349	11,206,847	Serb	Serbian Orthodox	New Dinar	Republic
SEYCHELLES	Victoria	176	456	76,164	English	Catholic	Rupee	Republic
SIERRA LEONE	Freetown	27,699	71,740	5,296,651	Creole	Muslim	Leone	Republic
SINGAPORE	Singapore	250	648	3,490,356	Chinese	Buddhist	Singapore Dollar	Republic
SLOVAKIA	Bratislava	18,859	48,845	5,396,193	Slovak	Catholic	Koruna	Republic
SLOVENIA	Ljubljana	7,821	20,256	1,970,570	Slovenian	Catholic	Tolar	Republic
SOLOMON ISLANDS	Honiara	10,985	28,451	441,039	English/ Pidgin English	Anglican	Solomon Islands Dollar	Parliamentary democracy within the Commonwealth of Nations
SOMALIA	Mogadishu	246,201	637,661	7,140,643	Somali	Sunni Muslim	Shilling	In transition
SOUTH AFRICA	Cape Town; Pretoria; Bloemfontein	471,008	1,219,911	43,426,386	English/Zulu/ Xhosa	Traditional beliefs/ local Christian churches	Rand	Republic
SPAIN	Madrid	195,364	505,993	36,167,744	Spanish	Catholic	Euro	Constitutional monarchy
SRI LANKA	Colombo	25,332	65,610	19,144,875	Sinhala	Buddhist	Rupee	Republic
SUDAN	Khartoum	967,493	2,505,807	34,475,690	Arabic	Sunni Muslim	Pound	Republic with strong military influence
SURINAME	Paramaribo	63,039	163,271	431,156	Dutch/ Sranan/Hindu	Hindu/Catholic/ Sunni Muslim	Suriname Guilder	Republic
SWAZILAND	Mbabane; Lobamba	6,703	17,361	985,335	siSwati	local Christian churches/ Traditional beliefs	Lilangeni	Constitutional monarchy
SWEDEN	Stockholm	173,731	449,963	8,911,296	Swedish	Evangelical/ Lutheran	Krona	Constitutional monarchy
SWITZERLAND	Bern	15,942	41,290	7,275,467	German/ French/Italian	Catholic/ Protestant	Swiss Franc	Federal republic

COUNTRY	CAPITAL	AREA SQ MI	AREA SQ KM	POPULATION	LANGUAGE	RELIGION	CURRENCY	GOVERNMENT
SYRIA	Damascus	741,498	185,180	17,213,871	Arabic	Sunni Muslim	Pound	Republic (under milita regime)
TAIWAN	Taipei	13,696	36,179	22,113,250	Min/Mandarin Chinese	Taoism/Buddhist	Taiwan Dollar	Constitutional monarchy
TAJIKISTAN	Dushanbe	55,251	143,100	6,102,854	Tajik	Sunni Muslim	Ruble	Republic
TANZANIA	Dar es Salaam; Dodoma	364,899	945,088	31,270,820	Swahili	Traditional beliefs/Sunni Muslim	Shilling	Republic
THAILAND	Bangkok	198,455	513,998	61,210,000	Thai	Buddhist	Baht	Constitutional monarchy
TOGO	Lomé	21,927	56,791	5,080,413	Ewe	Indigenous beliefs	CFA Franc	Republic
TONGA	Nuku'alofa	289	740	108,207	Tongan	Free Wesleyan	Pa'anga	Constitutional monarchy
TRINIDAD AND TOBAGO	Port-of-Spain	1,981	5,131	1,102,096	English	Catholic/Hindu	Trinidad and Tobago Dollar	Parliamentary democracy
TUNISIA	Tunis	63,179	163,610	9,513,603	Arabic	Sunni Muslim	Dinar	Republic
TURKEY	Ankara	301,382	780,579	65,599,206	Turkish	Sunni Muslim	Lira	Republic
TURKMENISTAN	Ashkhabad	188,455	488,098	4,366,383	Turkmen	Muslim	Manat	Republic
TUVALU	Funafuti	10	26	10,444	Tuvaluan	Church of Tuvalu	Australian Dollar	Republic
UGANDA	Kampala	93,070	241,051	22,803,973	Swahili/Ganda	Protestant/Catholic	Shilling	Republic
UKRAINE	Kiev	233,089	603,701	49,811,174	Ukrainian	Nonreligious/Russian Orthodox	Hryvnya	Constitutional republic
UNITED ARAB EMIRATES	Abu Dhabi	32,000	82,880	2,344,402	Arabic	Sunni Muslim	Dirham	Federation of emirates
UNITED KINGDOM	London	94,525	244,820	59,113,439	English	Anglican	Pound	Constitutional monarchy
UNITED STATES	Washington, D.C.	3,717,796	9,629,092	281,421,906	English	Protestant/Catholic	U.S. Dollar	Federal republic
URUGUAY	Montevideo	68,039	176,221	3,308,523	Spanish	Catholic	Peso	Republic
UZBEKISTAN	Tashkent	172,741	447,399	24,102,473	Uzbek	Sunni Muslim	Som	Republic
VANUATU	Port-Vila	4,707	12,191	185,204	Bislama	Presbyterian	Vatu	Republic
VATICAN CITY	Vatican City	109 acres	0	860	Italian/Latin	Catholic	Euro	
VENEZUELA	Caracas	352,143	912,054	23,203,466	Spanish	Catholic	Bolívar	Federal republic
VIETNAM	Hanoi	127,243	329,559	77,311,210	Vietnamese	Buddhist	Dong	Communist
YEMEN	Aden Sanaa	207,286	536,871	16,942,230	Arabic	Muslim	Rial	Republic
ZAMBIA	Lusaka	290,583	752,610	9,663,535	English/Bemba	Protestant/Traditional beliefs/Catholic	Kwacha	Republic
ZIMBABWE	Harare	150,803	390,580	11,163,169	English/Shona	Anglican/Traditional beliefs	Zimbabwean Dollar	Republic

Chapter 4

The U.S. in Focus

You live in the U.S., but how much do you know about it? Who are the movers and shakers who head the federal government's three branches? Which of the 50 states has a name that means "sky-tinted waters"? What territory did the U.S. buy from Denmark for $25 million?

If you don't know the answers off the top of your head, no problem. They are all in this table—Part 1 of the U.S. in Focus section. These three pages provide a wealth of information about the 50 states, the District of Columbia, and U.S. territories and commonwealths. Happy exploring!

Area: 3,536,338 square miles; ranks fourth[1] in the world.

Population: 291,950,153; ranks third[2] in the world.

Capital: Washington, D.C.

Form of Government: Presidential-legislative democracy. The U.S. Constitution divides federal (national) powers among three independent branches of government: the legislative, the executive, and the judicial. Powers not given to the federal government by the Constitution are held by the states.

State Name / Nickname	Origin of Name	Entered Union	Land Area (sq mi) / Population	Capital
ALABAMA The Cotton State	Named for Alibamu Indian tribes	1819	50,750 4,486,508	Montgomery
ALASKA The Last Frontier (unofficial)	Russian version of an Aleut word	1959	570,374 643,786	Juneau
ARIZONA The Grand Canyon State	Indian word *arizonac,* means *small spring*	1912	113,642 5,456,453	Phoenix
ARKANSAS The Land of Opportunity	From an Indian word meaning *land of downstream people*	1836	52,075 2,710,079	Little Rock
CALIFORNIA The Golden State	A treasure island in a popular Spanish tale	1850	155,973 35,116,033	Sacramento
COLORADO The Centennial State	Spanish for *colored red*	1876	103,729 5,506,542	Denver
CONNECTICUT The Constitution State	Algonquian Indian word; means *on the long tidal river*	1788	4,845 3,460,503	Hartford
DELAWARE The First State	Honors Lord De La Warre, first governor, Virginia Colony	1787	1,955 807,385	Dover
FLORIDA The Sunshine State	Spanish word for *flowery*	1845	53,997 16,713,149	Tallahassee
GEORGIA The Empire State of the South	Honors King George II of Great Britain	1788	57,919 8,560,310	Atlanta
HAWAII The Aloha State	Native word for *homeland*	1959	6,423 1,244,898	Honolulu
IDAHO The Gem State	Word invented to mean *gem of the mountains*	1890	82,751 1,341,131	Boise
ILLINOIS The Land of Lincoln	For Iliniwek Indians; name means *superior men*	1818	55,593 12,600,620	Springfield
INDIANA The Hoosier State	Word *indian* plus suffix *a*	1816	35,870 6,159,068	Indianapolis
IOWA The Hawkeye State	Indian word for *beautiful land*	1846	55,875 2,836,760	Des Moines

State Name / Nickname	Origin of Name	Entered Union	Land Area (sq mi) / Population	Capital
KANSAS The Sunflower State	For Kansa Indians; name means *people of the south wind*	1861	81,823 2,715,884	**Topeka**
KENTUCKY The Bluegrass State	Cherokee word for *meadowland*	1792	39,732 4,092,891	**Frankfort**
LOUISIANA The Pelican State	Honors Louis XIV, king of France	1812	43,566 4,482,646	**Baton Rouge**
MAINE The Pine Tree State	Honors ancient French province of Maine	1820	30,865 1,294,464	**Augusta**
MARYLAND The Old Line State; The Free State	Honors Queen Henrietta Maria of England	1788	9,775 5,458,137	**Annapolis**
MASSACHUSETTS The Bay State	For Massachusett Indians; name means *near the great hill*	1788	7,838 6,427,801	**Boston**
MICHIGAN The Wolverine State	Chippewa word *michigama;* means *great water*	1837	56,809 10,050,446	**Lansing**
MINNESOTA The Gopher State	Sioux Indian word for *sky-tinted waters*	1858	79,617 5,019,720	**St. Paul**
MISSISSIPPI The Magnolia State	Indian word meaning *father of waters*	1817	46,914 2,871,782	**Jackson**
MISSOURI The Show Me State	Indian word meaning *town of the large canoes*	1821	68,898 5,672,579	**Jefferson City**
MONTANA The Treasure State	Spanish word for *mountainous*	1889	145,556 909,453	**Helena**
NEBRASKA The Cornhusker State	Oto Indian word *nebrathka;* means *flat water*	1867	76,878 1,729,180	**Lincoln**
NEVADA The Silver State	Spanish word for *snow-clad*	1864	109,806 2,173,491	**Carson City**
NEW HAMPSHIRE The Granite State	Named for Hampshire, a county in England	1788	8,969 1,275,056	**Concord**
NEW JERSEY The Garden State	Named for Jersey, an island in England	1787	7,419 8,590,300	**Trenton**
NEW MEXICO The Land of Enchantment	Named for Aztec Indian war god Mexitil	1912	121,364 1,855,059	**Santa Fe**
NEW YORK The Empire State	Honors England's Duke of York	1788	47,224 19,157,532	**Albany**
NORTH CAROLINA The Tar Heel State	Honors King Charles I of Great Britain	1789	48,718 8,320,146	**Raleigh**
NORTH DAKOTA The Flickertail State	Named for Dakota Sioux Indians of the region	1889	68,994 634,110	**Bismarck**
OHIO The Buckeye State	Iroquois Indian word; means *something great*	1803	40,953 11,421,267	**Columbus**
OKLAHOMA The Sooner State	Choctaw Indian words *okla,* meaning *people,* and *homma,* meaning *red*	1907	68,679 3,493,714	**Oklahoma City**
OREGON The Beaver State	French word *ouragan;* meaning *hurricane*	1859	96,002 3,521,515	**Salem**
PENNSYLVANIA The Keystone State	Honors Sir William Penn (father of the founder of the colony), plus the Latin word for *woods*	1787	44,820 12,335,091	**Harrisburg**
RHODE ISLAND Little Rhody; The Ocean State	After the Greek isle of Rhodes (for its red clay)	1790	1,045 1,069,725	**Providence**

State Name / Nickname	Origin of Name	Entered Union	Land Area (sq mi) / Population	Capital
SOUTH CAROLINA The Palmetto State	Honors King Charles I of Great Britain	1788	30,111 4,107,183	**Columbia**
SOUTH DAKOTA The Coyote State	Named for Dakota Sioux Indians of the region	1889	75,896 761,063	**Pierre**
TENNESSEE The Volunteer State	From *Tanasie*, name of a Cherokee village	1796	41,219 5,797,289	**Nashville**
TEXAS The Lone Star State	From Caddo Indian word; means *friends*	1845	261,914 21,779,893	**Austin**
UTAH The Beehive State	Named for Ute Indians of the region	1896	82,168 2,316,256	**Salt Lake City**
VERMONT The Green Mountain State	French words *vert mont*; mean *green mountain*	1791	9,249 616,592	**Montpelier**
VIRGINIA The Old Dominion	Honors "the Virgin Queen," Great Britain's Elizabeth I	1788	39,598 7,293,542	**Richmond**
WASHINGTON The Evergreen State	Named after George Washington	1889	66,581 6,068,996	**Olympia**
WEST VIRGINIA The Mountain State	Honors "the Virgin Queen," Great Britain's Elizabeth I	1863	24,087 1,801,873	**Charleston**
WISCONSIN The Badger State	Chippewa word *ouisconsin*; means *grassy place*	1848	54,314 5,441,196	**Madison**
WYOMING The Equality State; The Cowboy State	From Delaware Indian word meaning *upon the great plain*	1890	97,105 498,703	**Cheyenne**

Capital District, Territories, and Commonwealths

Name	Origin of Name	Status / Date Acquired	Area (sq mi) / Population	Capital
DISTRICT OF COLUMBIA (D.C.)	Honors Christopher Columbus	Capital district[5] 1800[6]	61 606,500	**Washington**
AMERICAN SAMOA	Ancient Pacific deity	U.S. territory 1900[7]	77 70,260	**Pago Pago**
GUAM	From Guajan; in local dialect, means *we have*	U.S. territory 1898[8]	210 163,941	**Agana**
NORTHERN MARIANA ISLANDS	Honors Mariana of Austria, Regent of Spain	Self-governing commonwealth 1947[9]	179 80,006	**Saipan**
PUERTO RICO	Spanish for *rich port*	Self-governing commonwealth 1898[10]	3,427 3,885,877	**San Juan**
U.S. VIRGIN ISLANDS	Virgins of St. Ursula, early religious order; patron saint of Spanish sailors	U.S. territory 1917[12]	134 124,778	**Charlotte Amalie**

FOOTNOTES
[1]After Russia, China, and Canada. [2]After China and India. [3]A Jan. 30 election in Oregon will fill one Senate seat; a special election in California will fill one House seat. [4]I is for Independent (no political party). [5]Seat of the U.S. government. [6]Date when the federal government moved from Philadelphia to Washington. [7]Date gained by treaty with the U.K. and Germany. [8]Date ceded to the U.S. by Spain after the Spanish-American War; became a U.S. territory in 1950. [9]Date administration by the U.S. began (in a trusteeship for the United Nations); became a self-governing commonwealth in 1978. [10]Date became a U.S. territory; became a self-governing commonwealth in 1952. [11]NPP stands for New Progressive Party. [12]Purchased from Denmark for $25 million.

SOURCES
For nicknames, dates, entered union/dates acquired, and capitals: *The Book of the States, 1994–95* edition (Lexington, KY: The Council of State Governments, 1994) • **For origin of names:** *The World Book Encyclopedia,* 1992 edition • **For land area (1990):** *Statistical Abstract of the United States, 1995* (Washington, D.C.: U.S. Department of Commerce, Bureau of the Census, 1995). For population, 2002 Resident Population Estimates from infoplease.com, www.infoplease.com/states.html • **For governors/heads of government:** National Governors' Association, the U.S. Department of the Interior, and the Puerto Rico Federal Affairs Administration • **For U.S. senators and representatives:** *The Congressional Quarterly*

Index

Notes

Notes

Notes

Notes

Notes

Notes

Notes